MW00940100

A WALK THROUGH THE CHURCHYARD

TOWARD A SPIRITUALITY OF
CHRISTIAN DEATH

BY ROB GIESELMANN

Copyright © 2012 Robert K. Gieselmann

All rights reserved.

ISBN: 1480135070

ISBN 13:   9781480135079

Library of Congress Control Number: 2012919798
CreateSpace Independent Publishing Platform
North Charleston, South Carolina"

for Laura

THE READING MOTHER

I had a mother who read to me
Sagas of pirates who scoured the sea,
Cutlasses clenched in their yellow teeth,
"Blackbirds" stowed in the hold beneath.

I had a Mother who read me lays
Of ancient and gallant and golden days;
Stories of Marmion and Ivanhoe,
Which every boy has a right to know.

I had a Mother who read me tales
Of Gelert the hound of the hills of Wales,
True to his trust till his tragic death,
Faithfulness blent with his final breath.

I had a Mother who read me the things
That wholesome life to the boy heart brings —
Stories that stir with an upward touch,
Oh, that each mother of boys were such!

You may have tangible wealth untold;
Caskets of jewels and coffers of gold.
Richer than I you can never be —
I had a Mother who read to me.

— Strickland Gillilan

PROLOGUE

I hang suspended, floating as if in water. Gestation, slumber is amniotic fluid encasing me like a womb, the undisturbed sensation of eternal sleep; light and not blackness holds me. The light is not mere white but light incandescent and reflective, like sunlight after a spring rain, fresh and alive, when green leaves glow. I am dreaming.

From nothingness I *sense* sound. I do not hear it, this extraordinary sound, with vibrations and waves and color; no rhythm beats against my eardrums. The sound instead eddies somewhere above or below physicality, I'm not sure which, so my soul is transported either above or below physical acuity. My uninvited brain registers nothing. Only my soul hears.

I'm sure of it. My father is standing nearby.

My soul as seismograph perceives the tremor of his voice. *Daddy*. I always wanted to call him, *Dad*, but didn't have the nerve, and he never invited me to. I called him, *Daddy,* so that is who he was, even in this dream twenty-three years after he died. I had forgotten his voice long ago, its edgy tenor and southern quality. How could I possibly remember? He died when I was a teenager.

Yet, here, in this womb, I remember it, almost, I recognize it. It is as though I can grab and hold his voice in my palms, roll it between my fingers, draw it to my ears, and release it into my heart. I can own it. Almost.

But the voice dissipates and escapes. I neither own it nor actually *hear* it. It is instead some deep stirring or longing. It is both here and not here, a transient memory, an ephemeral ghost, the ashes of someone whose soul you carried intimately with yours, whose essence as a vine still entwines around you. You were part of each other, and you still are.

People, I think to myself, don't just leave when they die; they don't leave at all. People *live* through others, not just through a memory, but by becoming a part of the people they leave behind: woven fabric, fibers of steel, foundations, and essence.

Existential continuation, an existence that is vain, at best.

I don't often dream of my father, and I *never* hear his voice. Until this dream, I had lost his voice, my memory of him being only fabric faded by sun and daylight, an allusion to something that was.

Like when one of my children—was it eight-year-old Tate, or was it six-year-old Tilly?—said to me a year later, "I'm starting to forget what Momma looks like." Fabric that has faded.

Fabric turned brittle from wear and time and space. Fabric fades, and a memory isn't enough. Speaking through the souls of the living isn't enough.

Resurrection.

*Day by day remind yourself
that you are going to die.*

—St. Benedict

ONE

When Tate was six months old, Laura and I played *slip-n-slide*, skimming his naked belly, bottom-up, along the lines of the kitchen floor. We were living in an old house with high ceilings, yellow siding, and white oak floors. The farmhouse kitchen was built for gathering, and we spent most of our time gathering around the table. The kitchen was twenty feet long and twelve feet wide, and its ivory metal cabinets were an allusion to the time it was built, the steely 1930s. More recent owners had installed the gray vinyl floor and a large window that let in sunlight and made the kitchen a happy place.

It was a Saturday in 1995, and we were both home from work and bored. We had just eaten lunch, and one of us smelled Tate's poop. His diaper drooped to his rubber knees. I snatched the diaper bag from the dining room table while Laura sat down on the kitchen floor to clean Tate up. She pulled off Tate's dirty diaper, wiped what his younger sister would later call his "Crayola White" rear, and tightened the old diaper into a ball for the Diaper Genie.

While sitting on the counter by the kitchen sink, I watched the two of them, Tate and Laura. I considered Laura, and then naked Tate on the floor in front of Laura before she put a new diaper on him. I looked over at the sink and its sprayer, and then the idea came to me. I said to Laura, "Let's slide Tate."

"What are you talking about?"

I repeated myself, slower. "Slide him." As in water, as in spray water on the floor and push Tate on the vinyl.

Laura looked at me incredulously, with that *You're an idiot* look and shook her head. "No," and fished for a clean diaper in the bag.

"Oh, come on. Don't say no—just a little push."

Laura shook her head again, but not before I grabbed the sprayer and shot just a little water onto the gray vinyl right in front of Tate. The warm water landed perfectly, splashing him lightly. I hopped off the counter and knelt on the floor opposite Laura, pulling Tate gently to me across the water's surface. Laura cocked her head and looked at me. I swirled Tate around on the vinyl and water, gently, easily, spreading the water on the vinyl, and he giggled.

Now Laura shrugged her shoulders in tacit permission, neither committing nor resisting. She was five nine and thin, her strong jaw set forward, typically determined and edgy smart. Laura's "bedroom" eyes were brown and extraordinary. Here she seemed ambivalent, but she reminded me that she was typically anything but ambivalent when it came to her son.

"If you hurt my baby…"

I stood up, reached again to the sink, and sprayed more water onto the floor, covering about five or six feet. I sat down opposite Laura, again across the water, only farther away. Laura laid Tate stomach-down on the vinyl and moved his tummy as though she was moving a clock's big hand, in a circle so

2

the water would form a conduction layer between Tate and the floor. Holding one arm and one leg, Laura moved Tate a few inches to see if he would scream. He didn't, so she pushed him a little more toward me, not yet letting go.

Tate laughed out loud this time, so Laura slid him farther, more forcefully. Tate laughed harder, and Laura let go. He skimmed along the water easily, like a ballerina on ice. I caught him kindly and turned him back toward Laura. This time I pushed Tate harder than Laura had, and scooted back to enlarge the field. Tate sailed across the floor. He pumped his stubby arms gleefully, squealing and bobbing his head. His legs splayed, and now Laura started laughing. Me, too, we laughed at Tate's naked rear end, fat and shaking with delight.

Laura and I were not the perfect couple. Sometimes life devolved into a contest. Laura grew up as the baby in her family and adopted two approaches to life: fighting to get what she wanted and withdrawing. I am physically short and a scrapper. When people push, I push back, often argumentatively. People who don't know me assume I argue to be oppositional, but this is usually not the case. I argue because arguing helps me discover myself, helps me form opinions. When someone takes a position openly, I push back, to see whether their position is impregnable, to see whether it makes sense. I can't say Laura liked this about me, but she could hold her own. So no, we were not the perfect couple, but we were good together. Things worked between us.

I knew a month after we started dating that I would marry Laura. It was the spring of 1992. Both of us were in our early thirties. I was a practicing lawyer, and Laura was studying to take the CPA exam. We had become close friends during recent years, but I had decided I wanted more. After our first couple of dates, I knew we would marry. I saw it as destiny, God's hand, as though the plan had been made long before and we were simply living it. There was the love, too—love that coursed between us like some underground river connecting us to each other. To Laura, however, I needed to prove myself. She wanted to know whether I would stick by her. Until I proved myself, Laura would not know whether our relationship had legs.

I proved myself that June. Laura asked me to spend a week with her in South Carolina at her father's beach condominium on the Isle of Palms. Laura recruited her friend Kim to join us, in case things went sour. Laura tried to sabotage the week by pushing me away, hardly speaking to me, and drawing deeply within herself. Later, I learned that she was afraid of emotional intimacy and needed to know whether I would turn and run when things got tough. But I had come to love Laura, and I stuck by her that week and from then on. I stuck by her, and after that week, she was able to say with sincerity, "I love you."

Perhaps thinking of that first week at the beach, or knowing that Laura the homebody would never voluntarily explore new places, I proclaimed that all our vacations would *not* be beach vacations, that we were—by God—going to spend some vacations on adventures! And we did: the remote British island of Anegada for our honeymoon (still a beach vacation!), San Francisco and the northern Pacific coast, Victoria and the San Juan Islands. We traveled well together, and this first beach trip proved to be the only time a vacation would be difficult.

We were married Christmas 1992, in a beautiful yet simple ceremony at Sequoyah Hills Presbyterian in Knoxville. Laura asked our six nieces, all under eight at the time, to be her attendants. She dressed them in green velvet dresses laced with black, and they walked down the aisle on their toes, hesitant and tentative—so many eyes watching them. Laura's sister

Martha was matron of honor, and my two brothers, Butch and Pete, stood with me.

Laura's father, Lewis, hosted the reception at Club LeConte, and we danced to a jazz quartet that played "It Had to be You." An unimaginably long line of friends and family congratulated us. Laura greeted each person by name, and I would lean into Laura and whisper, "Who was he?" Or, "Who were they?" And I am still amazed Laura not only knew so many people, but recalled details about them.

We drove to Atlanta after the reception and flew to Anegada the next day. We spent a lovely week and our first Christmas at the beach, our second trip together. Laura gave me a shirt and sweater for Christmas, and we dipped fresh lobster in melted butter for Christmas dinner.

Perhaps it was on Anegada where we became so good together, or maybe it was part of the destiny to which I referred earlier. A good couple, and later, good parents, to both Tate and later Tilly. We were still a good couple nine and a half years later, in Maryland, when Laura died.

Laura died alone, in our bed, in the pale yellow room, while I slept downstairs on the flower-print sofa. That feather sofa was ugly and threadbare, and soft. I slept downstairs on the sofa because Laura chose to be alone.

I don't know why Laura chose to be alone. Maybe it was because she was uncomfortable after gallbladder surgery that afternoon, or because she was in pain from her reflex sympathetic dystrophy. Perhaps Laura needed the entire bed, not half of it, none of my bouncing and turning and shifting and snoring to wake her.

Or, maybe Laura just *knew* something. Maybe Laura knew she was going to die. Maybe she saw death lurking in the dark corner of the room. Maybe she just *knew*.

Whatever the reason, Laura died alone while I slept on the old flower-print sofa downstairs.

Looking back, I rather think Laura might have wanted company, someone to hold her hand, or to whisper, "I love you." But people die alone all the time, and some people choose to die alone.

A Kenyan once told me elephants die alone. They wander into the forest to be by themselves so they won't burden their families, or be an abstraction. Maybe Laura, as her last will and testament, simply wanted to save Tate, Tilly, and me from the abstraction of her death.

Behold and see where now I lye
As you are now, so once was I
As I am now, so must you be
Therefore prepare to follow me.

TOMBSTONE OF DANIEL COLEY, D. 1727
ST. PAUL'S CHURCHYARD,
BETWEEN CHESTERTOWN
AND ROCK HALL, MARYLAND

TWO

I like change. Moving to new places interests me. Unique and intriguing places, unexplored places, places with soul. I like the adventure of meeting people, making new friends, discovering the id of a town and its people.

Laura did not like change; she was a self-described home-body. "It's the Howards' fault," she would explain. "Only home is safe, and we don't like venturing far from home. We don't like change. Howards," she said a hundred times if she said it once, "like spontaneity only if you give us plenty of time to prepare for it."

Laura didn't say she wanted to stay in Tennessee. She didn't have to. She was a Howard. I will always wonder whether

Laura would have died if we hadn't moved from Tennessee to Maryland.

But, we were destined to move somewhere during that fall of 2001, and here the two of us were, four months before, considering the Episcopal rectory on Maryland's empty Eastern Shore—a fine place to die—wondering whether I should accept their call to ministry. Wondering whether we should say yes to this ancient congregation out in the country, *Old* St. Paul's Parish.

. . . .

The Episcopal Diocese of Easton has eight churches named *St. Paul's*. St. Paul's, Kent, is a brick battlement, its walls two, almost three, feet thick and made of fired English brick from 1711. The brick was shipped across the Atlantic and up a tidal creek that has long since silted so that shipping is now impossible. Slaves physically hauled the bricks from the barge to the church property.

St. Paul's is in the *middle of nowhere*, Laura and I told the kids before we moved, but someone must have thought it was *somewhere*. Maybe someone imagined a town springing up around the church. They built the church, but to this day, there is no town nearby. The closest is Fairlee, two miles away. People would tell me later, no other Episcopal congregation on Maryland's Eastern Shore has worshipped continuously in the same building for so long.

During the War of 1812, the Battle of Caulk's Field took place near Fairlee, and St. Paul's became a temporary hospital. You could hear the musket shots from the church, and medics carried the injured from both sides to St. Paul's and laid them on blankets on the pews. The dead were buried just outside, in the churchyard that surrounds the church.

There are nineteen acres of churchyard. A large millpond marks the eastern side of the property, where hundreds of Canada geese spend the winter. Great blue heron fish the pond, regal guards at water's edge. You can hear fox in the woods nearby, and in the summer, ospreys fly overhead, battling the bald eagle I've seen perched at the top of one of the dead trees.

The pond is shallow, and you can't swim in it. It is full of blacksnakes and snapping turtles. You can walk around it, or kayak it, and in the winter cross-country ski across parts of it. You can find your peace at the pond, which is meditation itself: quiet, yet extraordinarily alive.

Between the pond to the east and the church to the west are gravestones. People across the centuries left behind abbreviated records of themselves, names etched into marble stones, erased by wind and rain. Later, I would walk the churchyard to find solace, and the old stones would remind me of the old All Saints hymn: *one was a soldier; one was a priest; and one was slain by a fierce wild beast.* Unmarked graves, hold forgotten slaves, while ostentatious obelisks mark graves of once proud and prominent people, ironically also forgotten. God's people all, three hundred years of baptisms and burials from this little church in the country.

St. Paul's built the red brick rectory in the 1950s, about a hundred yards northeast of the church. A brick path leads from the church, among ancient boxwood, to both the parking lot and a driveway that circles past the parish hall and in front of the rectory.

St. Paul's is located halfway between Chestertown and Rock Hall. Chestertown is a small college town (Washington College). The big Episcopal church, Emmanuel, is located on the Chestertown square. A small *Williamsburg*, someone once described Chestertown, with its colonial buildings lining High

Street. Chestertown is proud of both its colonial and southern heritage, and maybe should be a little embarrassed over its own prejudices. Kindly old ladies would later lean into me and whisper about the women they hired to take care of dying husbands, "She's a *negro*," as though that explained things.

Rock Hall is located in the opposite direction, where Highway 20 dead-ends, heading westward into the Chesapeake Bay. Rock Hall started out as a fishing village. The old fishermen are called *watermen* on the Chesapeake; they bear leather faces and trap crab, harvest oyster, and catch rockfish. They are poor because the Chesapeake Bay is polluted and overharvested.

These days, Rock Hall is morphing into a sailing town, and now it claims more sailboats than people. The watermen don't fish much anymore; they dry-dock boats, and occasionally hire themselves out to clean gravestones at Old St. Paul's.

. . . .

Laura liked to tell the story of being left behind on a family road trip, and I wonder whether that might be why she became such a homebody. As the baby in the family, she was always stuck in the "way-back" of their station wagon on trips from Knoxville for vacations at Pawleys Island in South Carolina. Back then, Interstate 80 did not exist, and crossing the Smoky Mountains was difficult. The trip, winding up and down long mountain roads, was especially hard with children.

As Laura would tell the story, her dad, Lewis, would give each of the kids *one* bathroom permission slip. Laura would always use hers up by Newport, only one hour out of Knoxville.

Returning to Tennessee from South Carolina one year, they had just left the briny Low Country when Laura asked to take her bathroom break. Lewis stopped the station wagon at an old country store with warped floors and a sulfur smell.

Ten minutes later, after the kids packed back into the car, Lewis asked, "Is everyone here?"

To which her brother, Lew Jr., affirmed, "All here!" knowing Laura was still in the store.

Lewis drove on, and it wasn't until an hour later when he realized that he'd left Laura behind at the store! They turned around, drove the hour back, and found Laura with tears streaming down her face.

"You left me!"

As an adult, Laura would tease her mom, Anne, about those beach trips, Laura always the underdog. The four kids would bicker constantly in the back of the car, so Anne would swat her hand through the air as if at a mosquito. The older kids would duck, but Laura, the youngest, was always too slow. Anne's hand would find Laura's head, and she would yell out, "I didn't do anything," to which Anne would retort, "Well, you've done something to deserve it, I'm sure of that."

Maybe Laura inherited her dry wit from Anne, or maybe it was from Lewis, with his own intelligent and acerbic quips. When I "dragged" Laura off to seminary, she told everyone, "I wish he'd just bought a red sports car." Later, when money was tight, she would add with a lilt, "I married a lawyer." Meaning, not a priest.

Despite these one-liners, Laura endorsed my seminary venture. She wanted me to be happy, for us to be happy, and she knew we'd be happiest when each of us felt fulfilled.

As a teenager, Laura learned to play guitar on an Ovation, singing folk songs. Following high school, she joined Up with People and toured the country. Later, in her thirties, Laura took singing lessons from Aunt Peggy. Aunt Peggy helped Laura locate her crystal soprano voice. She would sing with her cousin Julie—Aunt Peggy's daughter—and at my ordination, they sang an extraordinary duet (was it *Panis Angelicus?*). Three years later, at Laura's funeral, Julie sang solo.

Tate was born a year and a half after Laura and I were married, and Tilly three years after that. Now, through some improbable wave of destiny's wand, here we were, on Maryland's Eastern Shore, far from Knoxville and Kenesaw Avenue, wondering whether we could find "home" in that particular rectory, at that particular holy place. Between Chestertown and Rock Hall.

Laura didn't want to leave Tennessee. She feared change. But on that unusual July day—it felt more like a Vancouver summer than a Chesapeake summer—as we looked out over the rectory's backyard, she knew. She knew. I didn't know. But she knew.

. . . .

The *Old* St. Paul's rectory is a two-story Cape Cod, only brick and not cedar shake siding, situated in the middle of the churchyard. The house looked like an old blind dog, worn and tired. Inside, cats had shredded the old pinched drapes, and the flowered wallpaper peeled back and showed dirt. The unit air conditioner stuck out of a hole in the wall to the left of the fire-place, near the floor. The living room was dank and smelled of mold. I was sure after walking through the house Laura would veto the move.

But we stepped outside onto the back patio, and looked through ripped screens to the lawn sloping downward to the millpond. We heard solitude whisper from either side of the churchyard. We sensed, then saw, an osprey hang above the pond, fishing. In the silence, absorbed by the silence,

12

something extraordinary happened to Laura, inside of Laura, the homebody.

Perhaps it was intuition. Perhaps it was a mother scratching for her nest. Perhaps it was a sense that this was her place. Her place of quiet, of peace. Her savanna. Whatever it was, Laura looked over the green lawn sloping toward the pond, grew quiet, then turned to me, and said, "This place is holy." This place is holy.

A holy place, a place of solitude, a good place to live. And a good place to die.

Though God be everywhere present, yet God is only present to thee in the deepest and most central part of thy soul.

—WILLIAM LAW

THREE

Some places are holy. Maybe they are holy intrinsically. Maybe they become holy by some blessing or sacred activity. Regardless of how or why, some places are indeed *holy*.

When Moses stood in front of the burning bush with his mouth agape, the bush warned him, "Take your shoes off; for you are standing on holy ground."

I remember visiting Dijon, France, years ago. I don't care much for most European cathedrals. They are extraordinarily beautiful and distant, ornate stone caves. The small cathedral in Dijon, France, is different. When I walked through its doors on a misty November afternoon, when I walked through its catacombs that had been there for centuries, perhaps even a millennium, when I slowly knelt to pray in the same spot where thousands of priests and people had offered to God petitions that were to them no small matter, then I knew — I was on holy ground. I found myself in a holy place. I could sense the depth of God hanging in the air, as if those who sought God, who longed to know God, their presence was still there, not as ghosts, but as holiness. As a spiritual presence, of a sort. Don't ask me to explain it, but it is true. I felt it; the holiness was painted on the walls.

Indeed, places can be *holy*. Some places express other personalities or characteristics, alive with feeling.

When Herod murdered John the Baptist, Jesus withdrew to what scripture calls, *a lonely place*. In that lonely place, Jesus found time—time to mourn, time to pray, and time to think. Time to be alone. A place where the people would not press in on Jesus, where they wouldn't extract soul from him. Jesus stole away to the eastern shore of the Sea of Galilee.

Lonely places are for mourning, for thinking, for searching one's soul. You visit a lonely place to *feel* God. And, you go to a lonely place to *feel* yourself. And Jesus found this lonely place to honor the lonely place in his heart, for surely Jesus felt alone after John died.

About a year after Laura died, I took Tate and Tilly to a remote part of Oaxaca, Mexico, to be alone. Oaxaca was *my* lonely place, partly because of its remoteness, but also because it offered cultural isolation. To truly escape, I needed to be in a different world, one without the intrusions of daily life, one without the tug of the news, or family and friends. In Mexico, I couldn't even carry on meaningful conversation.

Some places exist as if in shadow, like the room in which someone dies. Sadness occupies the room, casting an indescribable pall across it, a winter's steel day. The air weighs more in that room, and sometimes the room will stay that way for months, or even years, after the person has died.

What about magical places like the Garden of Eden, with the very stamp of creation upon it, the newness, the freshness?

Or dangerous places, like a desert? The desert is a void, a place even God avoids. The desert belongs to the devil, and there he holds his mirror to the human soul, revealing his demons.

I remember an all-night prayer vigil once, Maundy Thursday, the night before Good Friday; I had signed up for the predawn hour of six o'clock. At exactly six o'clock, I walked into the small redwood-paneled room, with its prie-dieu and makeshift altar, its cross veiled in black. Votives, as prayer, lit dimly the darkened room. All night people had knelt or stood or sat in prayer and contemplation and praise and worship in that space. But the room was not just a room in which people had prayed, it was a room that contained prayer. Walking into that room was like walking into prayer itself. Prayer as oxygen filled the room; a cloud, but there was no actual cloud. It was prayer. As I sat there contemplating the feeling of that place, I realized that it mattered less whether I pray than that I do nothing to dispel the prayer already there. Prayer was alive in that room.

Some places assume qualities unique to only one person. My father died after my first year in college. My mother sold my high school home and moved to a smaller house in another city. It was a new patio condo, perfect for a middle-aged widow living alone. Yet, that condo was never home to me. I had no roots there, no memories. No meaning.

I did have roots elsewhere: in Mim's house. My grandmother lived on Snowden Avenue in the same Memphis house that she had lived in for fifty years. It was an old twenties brick bungalow, with a big front porch and dormers sticking out all over its rectangular roof. As a child, I rode a trike into a wasp hive hidden in the English ivy climbing the brick columns on her front porch. I used to sneak into the attic and dig through boxes that, to me, were treasure chests, finding toys that had been my father's when he was my age, books he had read, and even Indian Head pennies. My uncle's old Lionel train set was still set up in the attic, seemingly acres in size, and I could run it whenever I wanted to. I'd send it going too fast into curves, and it would fly off the track.

Nothing ever changed in my grandmother's house, nothing. The same Oriental rug underneath the same black mahogany dining room table. As a boy, my father learned to play on the same spinet still standing in the corner of the living room, against the very same wall. If you moved that piano, you would have noticed that the wood underneath was darker, and the varnish thicker. To this day, I keep a bronze candy dish that Mim always kept on her coffee table. That dish has become my icon, my portal to Mim's house, even though she moved into an assisted-living facility twenty-five years ago and died soon after.

Places. Jesus withdrew to a lonely place, to escape, to be alone, to be quiet. To hear God; or maybe to complain to God. To feel what he couldn't feel otherwise, because the crowds intruded into his private world of struggles and musings.

God shows up in lonely and holy places; God takes evening strolls through lonely places. God hides in the crag of lonely places; God hides in the crag of the lonely heart.

And in places made holy because of people consecrated to God. Not perfect, but given. Christ's own forever. A place, then, is holy because the person standing on it is holy. Eternity.

Take off your shoes, then, for you, too, are standing on holy ground.

Just so, remote *Old* St. Paul's church on Maryland's Eastern Shore is holy. Not just the colonial brick box, with its simple altar window of jewels dancing as fire on the altar on spring mornings. Not just the pews, in which you can sense not just last week's worship, but last year's, and last century's. The pew doors open and close during Communion in the cadence of three centuries of pilgrims streaming to the altar with hands out, palms up, street people seeking nickels from God. Three hundred years of people who needed God, who loved God, in this very place. People who through three hundred years offered God their greatest sorrow, desire, or hope.

Not just the building, but the churchyard, too. Where husbands fought against tears and lost as they laid their wives down. Where wives, too, both those stoic and those given to emotion, laid their children's fathers down; and children, their parents, and parents their children. All looking to God somehow to ease the pain or to answer the question, *why?* And then later, perhaps a week, perhaps a year, strolling through the churchyard, between gravestones and oaks, spruce and boxwood, startled suddenly by the presence of the church itself, startled suddenly by the memory not of the death, but of the life. The birth, the marriage. The baptism, the wedding. Remembering the sweet, and not the bitter. And God attended both moments, both the burial and the resurrection, both the death and the life.

And so it is natural that Laura, looking out across the backyard, at blue herons wading across the pond, at the ospreys hovering, would whisper a simple truth about this place: "It's holy." For this place, you see, beckons the soul to God, implores it to turn, and see. To taste and *feel*.

Take off your shoes, then, for you, too, are standing on holy ground.

We must all die; we are like water spilled on the ground which cannot be gathered up. But God will not take away a life; he will devise plans so as not to keep an outcast banished forever from his presence.

2 SAMUEL 14:14

FOUR

I remember the first time I watched somebody die.

I was a seminarian. Seminarians must complete one unit of Clinical Pastoral Education (CPE), what is essentially an on-the-job training in sensitivity, a how-to course in counseling. The student learns and works with patients and their families in crises, often in death and dying situations. Most CPE programs are hospital-based, like mine.

CPE is designed to be stressful. Not only have students left their families—and often small children—behind; not only have they recently left jobs or careers to start this new life of ministry; not only have they just finished one year of a type of school in which professors dissect their faith like corpses at an autopsy; but they are forced into very real, painful, and difficult real-life situations with families who look to them for answers, answers that they might not have.

My own tension was compounded. Tilly, my daughter, was due to be born that June, during CPE. In retrospect, I have often wondered, *why do we set unseasoned seminarians loose on people who are dying?*

I took my CPE at Methodist Hospital in Indianapolis. At the time, Methodist offered a rigorous compact course that was only one month long. Most CPE programs are ten to twelve weeks in length. Methodist developed this program by promising the certifying board that we would work double shifts, sixteen hours each day, six days each week. If we missed any time, which I did when Tilly was born, we made it up by being on call during the remaining eight hours of some days, and on our day off.

The hospital assigned me to the cardiac care unit. The first thing I would do each day was go from room to room, checking to see if newly admitted patients with religious sentiments wanted to add prayer or conversation to their medical care.

The goal, we learned, was to let the patient's need guide the conversation, not our needs, despite the temptation to do otherwise. Each of us, clergy included, naturally projects our thoughts and feelings onto others, but projections do not help the person dying. She isn't likely to think and feel what we would if we were in her situation. The patient is a unique individual, with her own unique hopes, dreams, fears and hesitations, and should be treated and respected as unique.

On call one night, I was sent to the room of a woman dying of breast cancer. The family had asked for the on-call chaplain, who was I. I was still new to all of this. Methodist Hospital occupies several city blocks, so just finding my way to the room proved to be difficult. As I snaked my way through the empty halls—it was late—I prayed, *God, be with this woman as she dies. Watch over her; keep her; receive her warmly. Let her have peace, and no pain. And be with her family; soften their sense of loss with your kindness.*

I carried my Episcopal Book of Common Prayer, marked at both Last Rites and the Psalms. The book felt like a pendulum in my right hand as I walked, forward, backward, tick, tock. My left hand balanced my right as a shadow, a yin to my yang. I became acutely aware that I had no business taking God to the dying. I felt like Isaiah, a man of unclean lips.

As I turned the corner onto the patient's hallway, I noticed two or three people standing outside one particular room. One of the women stopped me. "Are you the preacher?"

I, of course, wanted to turn around to see who she was speaking to. Preacher? I'd delivered only one sermon in my life, quite mediocre. While I "preached," my son, Tate, who was two at the time, stood on the back pew and stared at me through his toy binoculars—only he stared through the wrong end, making me smaller than life, which is pretty much how I left the congregation that day, with the sense of having heard someone smaller than life. So no, I was no preacher. Yet, instinctively, I knew the woman meant *me*, the appointed *chaplain*.

"Yes," I answered. My voice cracked.

"Good," she said, monotone.

I followed her into the room, which was full of people standing around the bed of one gray woman, out cold. Her husband of forty years stood bent at her head. Her impending death was squeezing life from him. The others standing around the bed were her family, elbow to elbow, each breath their collective prayer.

I immediately wondered what use these seemingly kind country folk might make of me—this family just like any other family, with its good and its bad, its clean and its unclean. I didn't ask and just stood there, ready to pray for the dying, for the ease of this woman's pain, or their pain, pray for God's peace. Pray for something holy that might ease death's sting.

I took my place at the woman's head, opposite her husband. They waited a minute, and so did I. Finally, one of them, a daughter, looked me in the eye, and pointed at her brother standing at my right, the family's black sheep. "Johnny wants to get saved."

Did I hear her correctly? Johnny wants to get saved? Don't they want me to pray for their dying mom, or at least their grief-stricken dad? That is what I would have wanted, but my projections were not their need. Their need was for Johnny to get saved. Johnny, his sister went on to explain, needed to *get saved* because it was their mom's dying wish. She loved Johnny best, and she couldn't go in peace until he was saved. She needed to know Johnny had called a truce with God, yielded, trusted. That Johnny had finally stopped his drinking, card playing, and chasing after women. This was their analysis, not mine.

How is a good Episcopalian supposed to save someone? Why couldn't they have asked for Last Rites or Psalm 23?

Hear the need; fill the need. Okay, I can do this, I thought to myself. I stood back, examined Johnny from foot to head, and in a stern voice, asked him, "Is it true, you want to get saved?" He nodded his head. "Are you willing to change your ways? To give up what has held you back?" I still couldn't say the word *sin*. I am Episcopalian, after all.

"Yup," he answered.

"Now, Johnny, you can't do this just for your mother—it has to be for you. Has to be your decision," I lectured him in my best Southern Baptist tone. "Is it for you?"

"Yes," he answered. "I've known I needed this for a long time, now—just wasn't ready."

"Okay, bow your head and repeat after me. Jesus."

"Jesus."

"I confess to you that I have sinned."

"I confess to you that I have sinned."

"That I have not lived my life like I should have."

"That I have not lived my live like I should have."

I reverted to Episcopalianism. "That I have done those things which I ought not to have done, and have not done those things which I ought to have done."

"What?"

"That I have done wrong."

"I have done wrong."

"Forgive me of my sins."

"Forgive me of my sins."

"I repent."

"I repent."

"And I turn to you as my Lord and Savior."

"And I turn to you as my Lord and Savior."

"And give my life to you."

"And give my life to you."

"Amen."

"Amen."

The Book of Common Prayer calls this *amendment of life*, the very painful moment of complete surrender required to move mountains, the moment of decision when you alter your course, turn around, and walk in the opposite direction. Some people get stuck and cannot change. They refuse amendment; they refuse repentance; they can't admit failure. And that's too bad because they won't be saved. I don't mean eternally. They won't be saved from the malady of an empty existence. The faith of Christ, the faith of Jesus himself, the faith of rebirth is the antidote to the poison of emptiness. Johnny took this antidote and changed that night. Amended his life. Became Christ's own, forever. I don't know if his mother ever knew, whether she regained consciousness or died later that night. What I do know is that God sparked a fire in this man's simple soul.

Letting the patient set the agenda is crucial, this simple incident confirmed. Not my agenda—theirs. I hadn't learned this lesson yet, the first time I was with someone who died.

Each CPE student was assigned a unit at Methodist Hospital. Mine was the cardiac care unit. My job was to wander the hallways, sticking my head into new patients' rooms, introducing myself as chaplain, and generally getting to know both patients and staff. The problem was, the patients in my unit were comatose, either because of the trauma they'd experienced or because their doctor wanted them calm and had induced a coma by medicine.

I was on call that first evening of my CPE experience, and my first page came from my own unit, the CCU. The call identified the situation as a dying patient, but the family hadn't called for the chaplain; the nurse had. The nurse thoughtfully sensed that this family—a wife and adult daughter—needed a chaplain.

On my way to the CCU unit—which, by the way, was closer than the other hospital units, and I knew how to get there—I prayed. *Lord God, please be with this person in death. Give me your guidance, and your insight. Amen.* I couldn't pray more because I didn't know more. In retrospect, I would like to tell you that I let the rhythm of my shoes on the waxed floors become a prayer, a *pat, pat, pat* that God could interpret as prayer, and answer. Utterances too deep for words. But that wasn't the case. I prayed simply and hoped a simple prayer would do, that God does not exact the sacrifice of words to meet human needs.

I walked into the patient's room while the nurse was checking his respirations. The man's breathing was shallow, a broken rhythm, not quite gasping, but a breathing born of the practice of a lifetime, a habit not easily broken.

He was near seventy, and his wife, standing at his bedside, was about the same age. Their daughter stood next to her mom. Together they looked so pitiable, and I pitied them instantly. Neither the wife nor the daughter knew what to do, or how to act.

Neither did I. A person's death, you see, is as intimate as a kiss between lovers. I was a voyeur, watching this family's most intimate act.

The nurse left the room, leaving the situation to me. All I could do was stand there. I comforted myself with my CPE instructor's lesson that we are a *presence* more than anything else, and just being there is sometimes all it takes. However, I felt like a hollow promise.

I prayed as I stood beside the bed, but I spoke so softly that night, that God couldn't possibly have heard me. I do not remember what I prayed, and after praying, I shrunk into the corner, again telling myself that being unobtrusive was critical. I was a presence, I reminded myself.

The truth was, I was so unsure of my role as a chaplain, that all I felt was that I had absolutely no business being there, in that room, at that moment, in that circumstance. The man was dying, and he didn't need me to help him do it. The wife and daughter didn't know me, couldn't trust me, and had no idea of my agenda. They didn't need me to help them do their part, either. They needed something else. They needed someone else—perhaps the kindness and extraordinary grace of the one I purported to re-present, but not me.

During all of this, the man continued to pull death as oxygen into his lungs and exhale life. In, out, in, out, a rhythm, with each beat leaving doubt as to whether another would follow. Silence, deathly silence, hung between each. A tear dropped from the wife's eye, off her cheek, and onto the floor. His daughter held her father's hand. Waiting.

The nurse walked back into the room and saw me standing in the corner. She didn't disdain me, nor did she judge me. Perhaps she recalled being a new nurse, in the same circumstance, waiting the first time for one of her patients to die. She walked over to the bed and took the man's hand. She stroked his hand; she stroked his arm. Maybe she was taking a pulse, a blood pressure, but if so, it wasn't obvious.

Quietly, she looked over at the man's wife and asked her, "Are you ready?"

Can anyone really be ready for the death of a spouse?

"Yes."

Yes. That simple. I can live on. It is time, and I don't want him to suffer any longer. We will be okay, okay. Okay without him.

The nurse looked at the daughter. "Are you ready?" she asked. The daughter nodded.

Without permission, without asking, without knowing, this nurse felt the pulse of God and told the man, "It's okay. They're ready. They are going to be fine. You can go now." All the while stroking his arm, massaging their souls.

Like an angel, she disappeared from the room. Thirty seconds later, the man died. He broke the stilted rhythm of his breath, almost as if he might breathe again, but didn't. As though it were a choice—his choice—he gave up his ghost.

Feeling my sea legs stiffen, I moved forward to pray with them, which I did, praying for their comfort, and that God would welcome this man as one of his own. *Christ's own forever.*

Into your hands, O merciful Savior, we commend your servant. Acknowledge we humbly beseech you, a sheep of your own fold, a lamb of your own flock, a sinner of your own redeeming. Receive him into the arms of your mercy, into the blessed rest of everlasting peace, and into the glorious company of the saints in light. Amen. (Book of Common Prayer, p. 465)

A pinprick in the fabric of this universe opens, and the soul of man is pulled from this dimension into the next, from this world into the next. A veil somewhere is torn, top to bottom.

I don't know what time of night Laura died, whether at matins or laud or prime. I was asleep downstairs on the couch. I can't know whether Laura yielded voluntarily, or if she resisted. I don't know whether she gasped in surprise or perhaps anticipation. I do know that she wasn't sure she could hang on forever. Her pain was unbearable. And maybe, just maybe, she chose the cloak of night so she wouldn't have to explain herself, to me or anybody else.

Laura was the elephant when she knows it is time. She walked as one solitary into the dark night, and yielded.

In blessing the bread, Jesus left behind a token, a memorial—like a lover going on a journey, so whenever you look at the token, you will be reminded of their goodness and love.

—PELAGIUS

FIVE

I lost my wedding ring. We were new to The University of the South, Sewanee.

They call Sewanee "The Mountain." Maybe it is an allusion to Moses and the Ten Commandments, or a reference to white towers and academics. Most likely, "The Mountain" speaks to geographic location, that part of the Cumberland Plateau that, for all practical purposes, feels like a mountain. Sewanee sits astride a small part of the plateau, between verdant valleys of oak and maple and dogwood.

This unique geophysics makes you think you are going *up* a Mountain to get to Sewanee, reminiscent of the psalms written for pilgrimages *up to* Jerusalem. People make pilgrimages up to Sewanee, but there is more. Sewanee is a place of friends and families and discovery and life, a place for young people to come of age and older people to consider the things of God. You touch God on the Mountain. You touch God in the university chapel, and you touch God at the enormous white memorial cross at the edge of the plateau looking out at the western sky.

Both the University of the South and its associated town of Sewanee are known together as *Sewanee*. Sewanee, is one of only two colleges wholly owned by the Episcopal Church. The other is Kenyon College in Ohio.

I was a postulant in 1996 when we moved to Sewanee. A postulant is someone authorized by an Episcopal bishop to attend seminary. It is believed that the postulant has been "called" by God into ministry.

In 1996, there were eleven Episcopal seminaries in the United States. Most bishops tell their postulants which seminary to attend, but my bishop, Bob Tharp simply guided me through the process, letting me pick for myself. I considered three seminaries: Yale (Berkeley at Yale), Virginia Theological Seminary (Alexandria), and Sewanee.

I rejected Yale immediately when I read its brochure. Yale didn't mention either God or what academia calls "spiritual formation," describing instead its exceptional academics. This bothered me, and that is why I rejected Yale.

I didn't reject Virginia so much as choose Sewanee. I was a lawyer before seminary, and I had hoped to support my family during seminary by continuing to practice law part-time. One of my best clients was an agency in Middle Tennessee that was willing to place me on staff as in-house counsel for five to ten hours of work a week.

Laura liked Sewanee, too. It was closer to home—to Knoxville, and Kenesaw Avenue—for this homebody who did not like to stray.

Laura jumped way ahead of me in this seminary-call-of-God thing. I had thought about seminary once long ago, when

I was eighteen. I even talked to my bishop (of Florida) about it. I was in college at the time, and he told me that I would need to work for several years after college before he would consider me for postulancy. He told me he thought I should experience life, so I would understand parishioners better.

Meanwhile, my father died. I felt lost and joined a different kind of church, an evangelical fundamentalist church. Although I didn't stay in that church long, the dual experiences of the death of my father and the church left me struggling with the fundamental question of who God really is, and what does God expect of each of us. It took me far longer than the two years that my Florida bishop had envisioned to come to terms with God and my life. I opted instead for law, but practicing law proved unfulfilling. Laura knew this about me, so when I first broached the subject of "call" and of seminary (which by then was a forgotten subject), she not only supported me, she pushed me. She sensed it as "right" immediately, and looked back only when it came time to move.

Moving was hard, especially for Laura, and it would be each time we moved: to Sewanee, to Cleveland (Tennessee), and to Chestertown. Once we'd lived in each place for six months, once Laura made new friends and felt like the kids had settled, she found each new place to be good. We looked back on each town and home fondly.

In August 1996, we moved into a little white Sewanee bungalow, cozy upstairs because of the pitched ceilings and dormers, but drafty downstairs. The walls had no insulation and billowed in hard wind, expanding and contracting with each gust.

The *white house* faced south, and for two weeks in the spring, ladybugs landed on the front of the house to warm themselves in the sun. At first, the ladybugs were quaint, a sign of environmental balance, but they kept coming. They started crawling through doorjamb, then through cracks and window-sills, thousands upon thousands of ladybugs, like some horror movie. We used brooms to scoot the ladybugs out while they continued to force their way inside.

The yard of the *white house* was large, and I had to mow it. Deer nibbled at the azaleas along the back, and both Laura and I pushed Tate in the swing hanging under the big oak outside the back door. It was in this house that we learned that we would not conceive a second time, and chose to adopt. It was in this house that Tilly came to us, at the end of that first magical year of seminary. We didn't stay in the *white house* after my first year of seminary, but we were there for that one, the hardest and best. During that first year, we lived.

We lived life as if days were free and life was eternal. We made friends, invited them to dinner, threw a party. On New Year's Eve, we moved the same fading flower-print sofa and two huge wingbacks against the wall so Frankie Rodriquez could teach the rest of us to line dance. I have no rhythm, and kept bumping into Laura, who kept showing me what not to do. I never did get it. It didn't matter, for it was here, during that break, and during that night, that this place, Sewanee, became home for Laura—and for me.

Was it really John Lennon who said, *life is what happens while you're busy making plans?* Life was happening all about us, dripping from the rooftop as rain, braiding the veins of our souls with others', friends to friends, and for Laura and me, soul mate to soul mate.

Life is like that, with those married. Hearts braided into one. I think it was our second week at Sewanee that I lost my wedding ring. Laura had inscribed my ring and surprised me with it on the day we were married: *The Rob and Laura Show,*

12/19/92. After we were engaged, Laura and I would watch Nick-at-Nite. Nick-at-Nite aired old reruns of *The Dick Van Dyke Show*, with Dick Van Dyke as Rob, and Mary Tyler Moore as Laura. *The Rob and Laura Show.*

It was a beautiful Sewanee fall day. The leaves had started to change, but only at their edges, green lined with reds and yellows and oranges. I was riding my bike for exercise. I sped up Tennessee Avenue, turned left onto University, left again at the Fowler Center, made a loop around the married student barracks, and as I pedaled back down University toward Tennessee, I stopped to do a few pull-ups on the bars at the playground. I pulled the ring off my left hand and put it on a wood block by the bars. I forgot *The Rob and Laura Show*, if only for a minute, hopped back on my bike, and headed home.

It wasn't until later, while washing dishes, that I realized my mistake. I jumped back on my bike. I rode to the playground. I ran to the bars. The ring was gone.

Laura wasn't mad; she wasn't hurt. It was a stupid mistake, but she didn't say so.

Sometimes I pray for silly things, and sometimes I find answers. I wonder whether God likes to answer the silly prayers just for the fun of it—could it be that God is playful? I remember once praying with my high school friend Kim Wright when she lost her contact lens in a swimming pool. *God, please help us find the contact.* Really, now, a clear contact lens in a swimming pool. But ten minutes after we prayed, we found the lens. This is absolutely true.

And so I prayed. *God—please. I'd like it back. You know where it is. It isn't lost; it just isn't where I left it.*

The next day, Bob Hughes, our theology professor, called me. "Did you lose your wedding ring?"

"How did you know?"

"I got a call from another university professor, who asked if I knew of any new students who might have, with his or her spouse, the names Rob and Laura. I looked at our new student roster and saw your names."

I told Bob how I lost the ring. Bob became God's eyes, and the other professor, God's hands.

I still have that ring. I would have replaced it had it never returned, but it wouldn't have been the same. It wouldn't be the ring that attended Laura's and my wedding, or the ring that flew with us to Anegada for our honeymoon, or the ring that watched Tate be born, or the ring that held Tilly when she was but days old. Objects, like places, carry with them meaning, as tokens, icons, pieces of the heart.

That ring was a token, a sign of a pledge, or more, a sign of the braiding of our hearts, our souls, our very beings, one with the other. Two become one. That phrase from scripture is no sweet platitude. It is a description of what happens to two people, a natural growth.

I grew up in Vero Beach, Florida. My mom would take us to Pocahontas Park to play. We climbed on the Korean fighter jet that the Navy had placed in the playground for kids to climb in and out of, and we climbed the monkey bars, chasing each other. A tree guarded the edge of Pocahontas Park, or rather, two trees. Someone had planted two trees—some sort of tropical trees, maybe banyans—too close together, and as these two trees grew, their trunks grew into each other. At first, they just pushed against each other, but over time, as the trunks became larger and larger, they shoved into and became a part of each other, so that by the time I was a child playing at Pocahontas Park, the two trunks had become one. Two distinguishable trees, with one merged trunk.

Marriage is like that—two grow together into one, and it happens when nobody is looking. It happens over dinner and moonlit strolls. It happens during arguments and planning a future. It happens while you watch *The Dick Van Dyke Show*, and when one of you tries to teach the other to line dance. It also happens when the homebody gives up the security of her home because she knows that in order to thrive, you, her friend and husband, need to go back to school.

Marriage doesn't happen at the altar rail, in the artificial moment that you recite someone else's words: *"Repeat after me. I, state your name, do solemnly swear..."* Marriage happens to people, not because of people. By the time a couple makes it to the altar rail, they are or should already be married. The public aspect of promises recited before God is important; God's blessing is important. But make no mistake about it, if the couple is to be married, the two should already be joined, standing in front of the altar, as one. Conjoined trees.

Laura and I were friends long before we dated. We went to movies and dinner. We had a larger group of friends that would get together to play games—charades or Trivial Pursuit (I was good at charades and lousy at Trivial Pursuit; Laura was good at Trivial Pursuit and lousy at charades). We never dated, mostly because of me. Laura even asked me once, "Did you ever think about us—about us dating?"

She must have wanted to, but dating Laura scared me. I answered blithely, "No. Sure haven't."

Funny thing is, by the time I was ready to date her, about a year later, Laura wasn't interested.

"Nope," she told me when I asked. "It would ruin our friendship."

But I wanted us to date, so I begged. And finally, during January of 1992, I convinced Laura to let me take her out.

"Only not until after tax season," Laura the CPA declared.

I waited until April 16 for our first date, but when she drove me home from that date, and parked in my front driveway, and later started to get back into her Isuzu Trooper to go home, I opened her door, stood on my toes while I held on to the door (Laura was three inches taller than I am), and kissed her for the first time. The earth didn't shake; fireworks didn't pop. Instead, our trunks bumped into one other, and started to grow, each into the other.

By the end of that summer, in 1992, I knew we would marry. There was no issue; we didn't wonder "if" or "should we?" A wedding ceremony was necessary, if only to confirm what God had already done. We were already so much a part of each other that it would have been wrong not to memorialize our relationship in a marriage ceremony. Or, to make my point, by this time, I recognized that we were already married.

Frank Dunn is Laura's jeweler friend. Everybody should have a jeweler friend as good as Frank. Frank and his wife, Nancy, are now my friends. Salt of the earth. Frank has long gray hair pulled into a ponytail, and he makes jewelry to order. He doesn't have a storefront, but an office. A jeweler with an office, like an accountant. Nancy teaches school and has been a great resource when I have a developmental or education question about either Tate or Tilly. I trust her because I've met their kids—both young adults now—and have seen how good they turned out.

Anyway, Laura gave me Frank's phone number late in the summer of 1992. She wanted Frank to make any engagement ring I might buy for her. I met Frank and said I wanted to give Laura an antique diamond in a more modern setting. He told me what to look for, and I found an antique diamond with a "European cut." Frank showed me possible settings, and together we found the perfect one, adding sapphires to offset the white center of the diamond.

Even though Laura gave me Frank's phone number, I didn't tell her we were conspiring. I wanted to surprise Laura, but, in early September, Laura caught me by surprise.

"Have you seen Frank yet?"

It didn't occur to me that she was speaking of *that* Frank, and we don't have any other friends named Frank. I kept a straight face exactly because I had absolutely no idea what she was talking about.

"I don't know what you're talking about."

"Frank. Have you seen Frank?"

I knew by now what she was talking about, but I continued the charade. "I have no idea what you're talking about."

Laura got mad, hurt, I suppose, thinking I didn't care about her or our life together. I did, of course, but she'd figure that out soon enough.

Laura was taking me to Naples Restaurant on Kingston Pike in Knoxville for my birthday at the end of September. She reserved the special "blue" booth, an elevated corner booth with a curtain drawn for privacy. *"I love you with all my heart. Will you marry me?"* I imagined myself proposing, catching her off guard exactly because it was my birthday, not a day to propose. She thought I hadn't talked to Frank yet.

I picked her up in my Honda. The ring was in my pocket. I opened the car door for Laura. She looked down, into the backseat, where—because I had just been to Frank's that afternoon—she saw Frank's business card, face-up.

"You said you hadn't seen Frank."

Caught red-handed! I was dumbfounded.

"Sit down," I said, exasperated. She sat down in the shotgun seat. I closed the door. On my way around the car to get into the driver's side, I decided, *Well, there's no time like the present!* I opened the driver's door and sat down, one foot in the car and one foot in the driveway.

I proposed, right there, sitting in the driver's seat of my little Honda, Laura to my right, all to explain the presence of Frank's card. She said yes, and my birthday dinner became a celebration. The waitress offered us water, and Laura threw her hand into the woman's face and exclaimed, "I'm engaged!" Over dinner, we talked about life together, and a wedding, and children, and who we should tell first, and how, and when.

We didn't wait long to get engaged, so why should we wait long for the ceremony? We planned a big wedding at Laura's church, Sequoyah Hills Presbyterian, for right before Christmas. Laura wasn't showy, and even though we invited around four hundred guests, she didn't collect a huge panel of attendants. Her sister Martha was her matron of honor, and our combined six nieces (six at the time—seven now) dressed in dark green velvet dresses with black patent leather shoes, and from age two and up, walked Laura down the aisle. My two brothers, Pete and Butch, stood up for me, and on that sunny and beautiful December day, at eleven o'clock in the morning, Laura pledged her heart and soul to mine in the form of a ring.

My ring, with its inscription of *The Rob and Laura Show.* The show lasted almost ten years. Winter to spring, to summer and fall. Season after season, year after year. Through the birth of Tate in 1994 and the birth of Tilly in 1997. Through seminary and moving to Sewanee, vacationing on Isle of Palms north of Charleston, moving to Cleveland, and finally to Maryland. Year after year.

It wasn't easy. We sparred just as we celebrated; we struggled with each change in circumstance—each move, the birth of each child, each new development in Laura's neurological disorder. Life isn't easy. Marriage isn't for sissies. It is rewarding.

Marriage is rewarding in a way few people expect. It is rewarding because, in the end, after a year, or five, or ten—or, I suppose, fifty—love is transformed from feeling and infatuation
to description and existence. You are in love because you love
yourself, and your spouse has become a part of you. You are
two tree trunks surprised that they finish one another's sen-
tences, know one another's needs, understand one another's
hopes. You are as one. Time slows for those sharing trunks, for
time does not matter any longer; the seasons do not matter any
longer. Love is a description of eternity, not a feeling. Love is
the internal movement of neutrons and protons and electrons
that, despite flailing here and there, manage to hold the atom
together as a unit.

The vow is wrong, "till death do you part," for you don't
part at death. The other person doesn't leave you suddenly; they
are in your blood, your tissue, your soul, embroidered onto your
fabric. You have cell memory of your spouse. It isn't a matter of being married one moment and not married the next.
Your blood isn't cleansed of another's by separation. Just like
the marriage doesn't happen at the altar rail, neither does the
separation. You aren't married one minute, and then not the
next. This is true for all marriages ending, whether by divorce
or by death. One might ask the question of whether a marriage
can ever end, for won't your mate be a part of you forever?

The seasons measure time, but they aren't time. The years
measure time, but they aren't time. The earth rotates on its
axis, and each rotation is a day; the earth revolves around the
sun, and each revolution is a year. But the cycles of rotation
and of revolution are not time. Perhaps time would be better represented as a continuum, a straight line, with events as
points on the line—birth, graduation, first job, marriage, second job, retirement, death. But even time on a line bears no

relation to the connection of two people at their deepest level. Two people together season after season, fall to winter, to spring and summer.

Other objects and people witness this joining—the photographs, the gifts from one to the other, the children.

Laura gave me a special silver cross when I was ordained priest. It was a cross with two circles at its center, the place where you would find Jesus on a crucifix. The circles are the rings of marriage, overlapping for unity, and separate at the outside for individuality. Two individuals, joined. As one.

The cross wasn't a particularly pretty cross. It wasn't expensive. To the extent that it meant something to me, it meant something only because Laura gave it to me. I don't like wearing jewelry, so sometimes I wore the cross, and sometimes I didn't.

After Laura died, that cross, and not my ring, became the icon connecting me through the veil to Laura. I would lie in bed, unable to sleep, wanting to reach out to touch Laura, but knowing I couldn't. I would pray—to the extent prayer was possible—and need to know Laura was in God's care. Sometimes I would hold one of my kids on my lap, to comfort them, and they me, because something for both of us was missing.

But it was there, in the absence, alone in bed, that I would reach to my chest and take the cross in my hand and hold the cross. That cross rubbed between my fingers transported me or her—I don't know which one—to the other. Laura became present to me through that cross, and through nothing else.

I lost that cross. It was a year after Laura died, in June of 2003. The kids went to camp, and I was alone. I borrowed some friends' beach house and took a trip to Rehoboth Beach, Delaware. I went to the beach, swam, read, and rested. And I reached up at the end of a time as I sat on the beach, to touch the cross, to touch Laura, but it was gone. The cross was gone. I jumped up from my chair, dug desperately in the sand. The people around me must have thought I was crazy. Then I ran to the ocean—surely it washed up on shore, I hoped. A contact in a swimming pool, I remembered.

And so I prayed. Again, desperately. *Lord, please...*

But God was deaf to this cry, and the cross that was my icon to Laura was gone forever. The contact lens was found; the ring was found; but the cross was not found. And neither was Laura. Laura is gone now. And like Mary at the grave, I wonder, *They have taken my love, and I do not know where they have laid her*.

Death is hiding in the corner of the blanket.

—Basotho (African) proverb

SIX

Tilly, 2005

Only cats are reincarnated. Not ferrets. Not people. And certainly not dogs. Only cats. I know this because Pepper told me so. People say cats have nine lives wrapped into a furball that has only one life, nine lives between one birth and one death. They're wrong. Cats are reincarnated.

Like I said, Pepper told me this. Pepper is my cat.

Momma gave me Pepper when I turned five. It was my birthday. I'm almost eight now, and that was three years ago. I don't remember that far back, not really. I don't remember Pepper as a kitten. She must have been a kitten. But she's not one now. And I don't remember her being a kitten. My daddy says she was. He also says that when she was a kitten, I held her all the time. I carried her everywhere. Daddy laughs, and then he tells me that back then, Pepper was little.

But I carried Pepper the same way after she got bigger. I still carry her that way. I hold her under her arms, and her bottom swings from side to side. *Swish, swoosh.* But Pepper doesn't mind. She's my cat. I'm her person.

I tell Pepper secrets. And when I am lonely, I tell her that, too. And when I miss Momma, I tell Pepper. Sometimes I tell Daddy. But mostly, I tell Pepper. Pepper understands. I know she does. She doesn't have a mommy, either. So I tell her that I miss Momma.

And it was one of those days, when I was telling Pepper about Momma, and how Momma would read to me, and how she taught me the alphabet, and how she made me practice my letters, and how I would snuggle next to Momma on the big red couch. *That* Pepper told me. "Cats," she said, "are reincarnated."

"Re-catnated?" I asked.

"Rein*car*nated," she said.

"What's re-incartated?" I asked.

"You know. Reincarnated. When you die, you get to live a second time. But you aren't yourself. You are someone else."

"Someone else?"

"Someone else."

"How can you be someone else?"

"I don't know. You just are," Pepper said.

"You die, but you aren't dead?"

"Nope."

"But you aren't you, either?"

"Nope. But it won't happen to you. Only cats."

Well, I thought about what Pepper told me. I thought about it a bunch. Because I wanted Momma to be alive still, but I didn't want her to be somebody else. Daddy told me that Momma is still alive. Somewhere. And that she is herself. When he told me she had died, he took me to her. He said something about saying good-bye. We walked into the room, and there she was, right in bed. I saw her. She wasn't somewhere else. She was in bed.

I told Daddy that she hadn't gone anywhere. "Look, Daddy! She didn't die. She's right there." Why would he tell me she was dead when there she was, right in front of me?

And he said, "Tilly, that's not Momma anymore. She's gone somewhere else. So you can say good-bye, okay?" His eyes were red.

I said okay because I didn't want Daddy to get mad at me. But I'm still pretty sure that was Momma. I try not to think about that day much, because that was the day Tate yelled and Daddy cried. And it was the last day I saw Momma.

The next day, when nobody was watching, I snuck into Momma's and Daddy's room to see if Momma was still there. She wasn't. I snuck in the next day, too. I still sneak in sometimes when I'm extra sad. But she's never there. Why did she leave? Without saying good-bye? She was there. Then she wasn't. Why did she have to go?

I don't know whether Pepper's right. But I know Pepper isn't Momma re-incatnated. She can't be. Pepper was born before Momma died. Besides, Momma didn't like cats much. Cats are my favorite, and when Tiffany's cat had kittens, I asked Momma for one. She looked funny. She said we'd talk about it later. She didn't feel good.

I asked her again the next day. "Momma, can I have one of Tiffany's kittens?"

"I'm still thinking about it, Tilly."

And the next day. It was the day before my birthday.

"Maybe," she answered.

I knew "maybe" meant I'd get one, so I ran off to tell Tiffany. I already knew which kitten I wanted. But then Momma died. She died before Pepper's eyes opened.

"I was Cleopatra's cat in one life," Pepper told me. I wonder if that means I'll be a princess, or a queen, when I grow up. I have Cleopatra's cat. Daddy calls me "Squirt." I told him I want to be called "Small Fry." He also says I'm his princess. If I become a real princess, Pepper will be a princess cat. Lucky Pepper.

On my birthday, Reenie came to visit. Reenie is my grandmother. I used to have two grandmothers, but Grandmomma died. Tate said she became a new star. Anyway, Reenie came for my birthday. Her friend Marty came, too. Momma fixed supper for all of us, and she ate, too. Then she got sick. She couldn't eat much. Daddy says that is why she had to have the operation.

I got to open all my presents after supper. And that's when Momma promised I could get Pepper. "You can have her," Momma said.

"Really?"

"Really."

At my birthday, Reenie and Momma, and Daddy and Marty, all sat on the screened porch. Tate and I played on the swing set. They talked about stuff—you know, adult stuff. I don't remember. I didn't listen anyway. But it was fun, and now, when I'm lonely, I try to feel that day all over again. I was getting my first cat. It was my birthday. I could hear Momma talk. I remember that she talked, but I don't remember what she said. I don't even remember what her voice sounded like. You can't catch a voice, you know. Daddy told me that. I can only remember what she looked like if I hold a picture of her. I keep one on the table by my bed. But I remember I felt giggly all day. And when I'm lonely, Pepper still asks me, "Tell me about the day I became yours." And I tell her about that day. It was my special birthday.

Farewell, friends! Yet not farewell;
Where I am, ye, too, shall dwell.
I am gone before your face,
A moment's time, a little space.

—FOR DEATH

Now I know, is that first breath
Which our souls draw, when we enter
Life, which is of all life centre.

FROM "AFTER DEATH IN ARABIA" BY EDWIN ARNOLD (D. 1904)

SEVEN

Death, as a blip, flashes unannounced onto your radar screen. An intuition deep within whispers, *It's time.* It is for you no longer distant, no longer for someone else, no longer for the stranger on the sidewalk. Death is calling your name.

How do you live life with death's overlay, its haunting voice? How do you say your *good-byes* to those in your life? *I love you?* Or do you lie to yourself, tell yourself that your intuition is foolishness? Do you pay your bills, buy more groceries? And then, when he's asleep beside you, reach through the darkness to touch his hand, as if to say *good-bye?*

It wasn't as though Laura knew she was going to die, at least not consciously. Yet, I wonder. I wonder whether death, as a blip, flashed onto her radar screen, whether her deeper intuition toyed with her: *It won't be long.*

During seminary, some my classmates and I engaged in a running debate: what did Jesus know, and when did he know it? Well, what about Jesus? When did his intuition whisper? When did the blip flash onto his radar screen? When did Jesus hear death call his name?

Luke tells us that Jesus set his face resolutely toward Jerusalem. Did Jesus actually know that he would die in Jerusalem, and if so, when did he figure this out? In the synoptic Gospels, Matthew, Mark, and Luke, Jesus' ministry was one long travelogue full of exciting miracles and right-between-the-eyes teachings. Jesus was a persistent traveler: he was a pilgrim aiming for the Temple, the racer determined to reach a Jerusalem finish line. Jesus put his head down as if in a storm. He pushed his way forcefully to that mile-high city, step upward by step upward.

But, did he know he would die there? Or, did Jesus perchance travel the countryside as a circuit king, an upstart monarch, expecting Jerusalem to crown him as its new David? Jesus acted the monarch's role.: he rode a donkey into Jerusalem, to great fanfare: "Hosanna! Blessed is he who comes in the name of the Lord! Hosanna!" They threw their cloaks onto the dirt in front of him, waved branches, and sang praises.

With authority, Jesus immediately crashed the Temple party of commerce and contrived spirituality. He whitewashed the Temple of generations of filth, moving from merchant to merchant, flinging doves and pigeons and coins skyward. "You have made my Temple a den of thieves." Next, Jesus scrubbed the Temple of its deeper filth, those who hawked their spiritual wares in the name of God, rabbis who exacted a price too high for the average consumer, lawyers who blocked everyday sons of Abraham from God, impeded simple and pure worship by constructing impossible requirements. The vineyard was truth, and Israel the vine keepers. Jesus told the vine keepers that God was giving the vineyard to others—people who would free truth, not prostitute it.

While Jesus cleansed the Temple, did he realize that the deepest cleaning was yet to come, at the price of his own life? Did Jesus *know* he was going die? To be rejected by both the political and religious leaders, and ultimately tortured and killed in a horrific and humiliating crucifixion? Maybe his was just an *inkling*—that whisper deep within, a foreboding, an impression of Jerusalem as dark and uninviting.

To be sure, the synoptics speak of Jesus' foreknowledge. "The Son of Man is to be betrayed into human hands, and they will kill him…" (Mark 9:31). Jesus was on his way to Jerusalem to suffer, die, and rise again, claim the Gospels, but hindsight is twenty-twenty, and these passages are church retrospectives. They were written at least thirty-five years after Jesus' death, giving the church plenty of time for a rear view look at Jesus' intimations. Indeed, Jesus may have seen his future with clarity, but more likely, he only expressed a sense of foreboding—a vague notion that something not so good was going to happen in Jerusalem, statements the early faith community interpreted as fortune-telling. Jesus' palm had a short life line.

Why do I believe this? Faith is a two-sided coin: heads, and you have a compulsion to act, and tails, you have resistance and doubt. Faith is neither absolute knowledge nor complete assurance. By its very nature, faith means you live in a state of unknowing, and whatever else you might say about Jesus, he lived a life of faith.

Jesus was also human. To fully identify as human, he had to be finite—a small part of the whole, a microcosm in the macrocosm. I cannot identify with, understand, or need a Jesus who hasn't wrestled in the universe of the incomplete, who didn't live a life of unknowing, just like I do. This shroud is the human condition, the soul's blanket. A cloud of unknowing later acknowledged by Paul: "Now we see in part..." For Jesus' to have been a walk of faith, he simply could not have known the future.

Jesus was human, but a human with the spark of the Divine. He engaged faith, lived faith, wrestled with faith. He was at once Abraham and Jacob, the friend of God and the God-wrestler, and his was a confidence, the prize of hard-fought battle. He sharpened his trust as a sword on life's whetstone. His faith-sense, his God-confidence, warned him against Jerusalem, but his Father promised something greater. Faith exacted its ultimate due from Jesus, complete reliance, to hell and back.

What did he know, and when, then, did Jesus know it? Somewhere along the line, Jesus realized that the end was an early death, at least the end of his earthly journey. When did this dawn upon him? Did Jesus have a dream that laid out for him a map of the unfolding events? Surely it is not possible that Jesus was so different from you and me. More likely, an evolution took place inside of Jesus – that life was not going to continue as it had for these three years, that the promise of life for others could only mean death to himself. My experience of God is that plans are never laid out in advance; we cannot look at life as a map. Not for us, and not for Jesus. Life unfolds.

Laura did not necessarily know she was going to die that day, that year, but she suspected that RSD would cut her life short. RSD is short for reflex sympathetic dystrophy, a horribly debilitating neurological disorder triggered by an injury to a limb—almost any type of injury will do. When the injury occurs, the sympathetic nervous system does what it's supposed to do: it sends blood to the injury to cleanse it. Next, it stops the blood flow to allow clotting. At this point, with the blood flow interrupted, the problem starts. The sympathetic nervous system finds itself in some sort of computer loop it can't escape; it refuses to reopen the blood flow to the injured nerves. Without blood's life-giving oxygen flowing to the nerve extremities, a horrible, bloodcurdling pain sets in. Over time, the sympathetic nervous system shuts down blood and oxygen flow to nerve endings nearby, spreading the disease, and then, in some people, like Laura, the problem spreads to other limbs.

The pain is often unbearable; morphine doesn't help. On more days than I can count, Laura lay on the couch, writhing in pain, and there I was: impotent. There was nothing I could do. I've had kidney stones before, and I could see my worst pain in Laura's eyes on those bad days. Kidney stones pass.

Laura's onset injury was an operation to her foot. Actually, she had RSD once before—she caught it early enough to tame it with spinal injections. Spinal injections are the miracle cure for those patients lucky enough to have a doctor diagnose their RSD early. Because of her first bout with RSD, Laura never should have had her foot operation, but she did. This time, nobody caught the RSD early enough for injections, and it took over her life. It took over our life.

The disease developed from there, and by the time we stood on the patio of the screened porch of the rectory, Laura needed a wheelchair to navigate the grocery store and the mall. Laura bought a used Chevy Suburban to haul the scooter. At the time, only a Suburban could carry a scooter inside without modification. After moving into the Maryland rectory, climbing the stairs became so difficult that Laura asked the church for a stair-well escalator. We never got around to installing one.

It wasn't Laura's debilitations, or even the pain, that were the hardest. A sense of death overshadowed Laura's life. RSD is not typically life threatening, but we could not imagine a life for Laura consisting of thirty, forty years of daily pain like hers. We talked about it.

"I can't live like this," she said one day, after a few days of the intense, toe-curling, sofa-only pain.

"What do you mean?"

"I don't know how long I can do this."

I had no answer, no false promise for her. "I know."

But I didn't know. Nobody can really know another's pain. We estimate another's pain based on our own experience. We project our pain, as though my kidney stone pain was her pain, but she didn't have kidney stones. She had RSD. Some people have a high threshold for pain. I don't. Laura did. When she made kidney-stone-like faces, I could tell that her pain was worse than my kidney-stone pain. Laura's doctors typically dismissed her pain, probably because they couldn't fathom it. Her pain was not in their dictionary. But the pain was real. I watched helplessly, as one watches a friend dying of cancer.

"Someday...well, I may...but I couldn't, not with the kids. Not now. But, someday."

I knew what she meant. I nodded. Someday.

I had always opposed the concept of mercy killings, Dr. Kevorkian, and assisted suicide. When Laura and I were engaged, we visited her mother and stepfather, Anne and Jack. Anne and Jack had both endured tough relationships, and per-haps only as the wounded can, found comfort each in the other. Old shoes, maybe. They had retired from Rochester to South Carolina, where they lived unpretentiously a few blocks from the beach. Jack helped save endangered leatherback turtles. Anne smocked dresses and knit baby blankets.

It was the Friday after Thanksgiving. Thanksgiving turkey and stuffing always tastes better on Friday than at Thanksgiving dinner. Pecan pie isn't better the next day; it isn't worse, either. Pecan pie is good any day. There was only enough leftover pie for everyone to have one piece. I have this irritating habit of leaving bites of food on my plate, of putting my fork down without scraping my plate. I leave bits of roll, clumps of meat, spoonfuls of casserole. I even leave small bits of pecan pie on my plate. Anne did not understand. She would clean her plate; she practically licked her plate. Not that Anne was overweight; she wasn't. She was thin; she had a remarkable metabolism and a love for pecan pie. She barely knew me, and certainly not well enough to ask if she could eat my table scraps. I noticed Anne looking at my plate, with its crumb shards, for about ten minutes while we talked about—well, who remembers? Finally, Anne asked, "Are you finished eating?"

"Yes," I said, curious, of course.

"Do you care?"

"What?"

Laura answered for me. "Go ahead, Momma. He always leaves something."

At that, Anne leaned forward and across the table, stabbed at the shards of pie, and ate them.

Maybe it was over that meal, or maybe it was at another meal that weekend, but sometime over that first real visit with my future mother-in-law, Anne told me that she was a member of the Hemlock Society. Until now, I had thought of the Hemlock Society as some sort of dark Roman/Caesar/ Brutus Shakespearean group that tried to glorify suicide. Suicide is wrong, I always believed. I didn't think of suicide as a coward's escape, but shouldn't we trust God with life's end? My thinking on suicide was immature, and when it came to physician-assisted suicide, well, I thought Dr. Kevorkian even looked like death. He had sunken dark eyes and sallow skin, a soldier of death. He seemed like the kind of guy who might be a tad eager to flip the switch, offer the pill, slip the morphine.

I was surprised by Anne's position, mostly because in my small world, I couldn't imagine a rational, educated adult not being exactly like me—middle-of-the-road conservative southern American, and therefore morally against suicide of any kind. It wasn't as though I imagined suicide to be a mortal sin. The so-called Christian who thinks God kicks a person when he is down, well, that person serves a different god, a harsh and cruel taskmaster.

But God sides with life, always life. Facilitating death cheats life, steals from it, decapitates it. Suicide seems so obviously the antithesis to life.

Maybe I am timid. Maybe I wanted to get along with my future mother-in-law. For whatever reason, I didn't take up life's cause with her. I didn't pick a fight. I ignored Anne's comment, but I remembered it clearly when Laura raised the issue later, about herself.

I had changed by then. Laura's pain changed me. Intuition was now my teacher, and I knew—I just knew—that for Laura, with her pain, with her life, the day would most certainly come when she would find life in death more than she would find in life.

I never quite said that to her, at least not directly, but we reached tacit agreement that day as we sat together in the living room. "We'll figure something out," I answered her. "We'll figure something out."

She knew I meant I would help her if she asked me to. I didn't want to. But I would. It would be my Christian responsibility. The sad duty of love.

We saved the almost-discussion we'd had for another day. Laura was Tate's and Tilly's mother, and in Laura's words, they needed a mother. Herself, she meant. She didn't know how long she could endure the pain, but she loved Tate and Tilly more than life or death. Perhaps closer to any Christ-pain I've witnessed in my life, she would have continued to endure her pain because she loved those two so completely.

I know now that, in one odd way, God exacted the same faith from Laura as from Jesus. Was Chestertown Laura's Jerusalem? Did she know she was moving to Chestertown to die? More to the point, was Laura aware that God had heard her unspoken prayer?

During her last six months, after we moved into the rectory, Laura gave more. She gave more to Tate, reading hours upon hours to him, and letting him read to her. They sat, with her in her spot on the sofa, often in pain, and Tate next to her, sharing stories of medieval knights and magical sorcerers, of boys and dragons, of shipwrecks and pirates. They made up word games only they knew, like the only two members of a secret club.

Laura taught Tilly the alphabet, read rhymes to her, and touched her face with her hand—memorizing it, I think. She would take Tilly's tiny fingers and run them along the letters so she would learn the shapes and sounds of social intercourse. And before she died—the week before she died—Laura painted on Tilly's wall a mural of fairies hiding in grass along a fence post, fairies to dance above Tilly's head at night so she would dream of her mother, so she would remember the promise she had made so often to Tilly: "Forever and always will I love you."

When we arrived at the hospital for Laura's gallbladder surgery, the day surgery that killed her, she asked me to pray for her. I had always tried to be a husband and not a priest to Laura. When I would pray for Laura, I would pray as a husband, and not as a priest. But that day, Laura wanted a priestly prayer. She wanted a blessing.

"The Lord bless you and keep you; the Lord make his face to shine upon you and be gracious to you; the Lord lift up his countenance upon you, this day and forever." I said, "forever," as I placed my thumb upon her forehead and made the sign of the cross. An hour later, before the doctors administered anesthesia, she looked up at me from the gurney and whispered simple words that I dismissed. I won't tell you the words now, but later. But this is my question: she knew; how could she?

Standing on the patio of the rectory that day, did Laura anticipate her death then at St. Paul's Church, as Jesus anticipated his at Jerusalem? With acquiescence—*It is all in God's hands now?* Was there not that vague sense of dying in the midst of living? Or living in the midst of her dying? Not absolutely sure of the future, but wondering, imagining, *How long?* What did she know, and when did she know it?

Once, in February, four months after we'd moved to Chestertown, and three months before she died, Laura told me that she had just heard about a teenage girl with RSD who died unexpectedly from a related heart issue. RSD doesn't affect the heart, say the doctors. But it does. At least for some patients. It attacks the limbs, and then the body trunk, affecting organs, including the heart.

Laura told me, "It is in my organs."

I didn't like that news, so I ignored it. I was tired of the evil progression of the disease, and besides, what could I do? "Hmmm," I answered. Hmmm, indeed.

"I'm going to ask Dr. Ferguson to check my heart."

"Okay."

And she did. Nothing turned up, at least nothing serious. But somehow, she knew. A person often knows more than tests reveal. Broad and wide was her awareness; it encompassed more than physical knowledge, and at some level, Laura knew. She just knew.

That's why she planned our trip to Disney World so carefully. She had always wanted to take Tate and Tilly to Disney World, but we decided to wait until they were old enough to remember. Tate was old enough to remember, and he will. Tilly, well, she wasn't yet five, so who knows what she will remember from that trip only one month before her mother died? But this was the year, Laura insisted. I would add in retrospect, *because she knew*. She stated plainly, "I want to be well enough to see them enjoy it." She knew. At some level, she knew.

Planning a future for her nestlings without her, and yet with her: the memories of something good, something pleasant. Disney World. We still take turns wearing the Goofy hat with floppy ears, the one Laura wore in the Florida hospital. We have pictures of her wearing it, and the hat reminds us of that trip, of Laura.

Home. A warm place of the heart's welcome. The mural. Sitting together on the sofa reading of pirates and knights and magical worlds. Learning the alphabet together. Home—the place, as someone said, where the small are great, and the great are small. Laura knit her hatchlings' nest with a love expressed in anticipation of something, for she sensed, as Jesus, that something greater than she was operating and that Jerusalem and time were drawing near and short. Faith, not to turn around, but to steel herself moving forward.

And I wondered, didn't I, that first week after Laura died, whether perhaps it was God's grace for her that she died, because of her pain? But only bifurcated grace, because it wasn't grace for me, or for Tate or for Tilly. God's grace in half-form. How can that be?

But I never wondered whether she knew. Something deep inside Laura had told her it was time. The blip of death flashed, and she yielded. The elephant turning consciously toward the savannah.

He who died at Azan sends
This to comfort all his friends,
"Dearest friends, it lies, I know
Pale and white and cold as snow
and ye say, "Abdallah's dead!"
Weeping at the feet and head
I can see your falling tears.
I can hear your signs and prayers,
yet I smile, and whisper this,
'I am not the thing you kiss,
cease your tears, and let it lie - - -
It was mine — IT IS NOT I."

FROM "AFTER DEATH IN ARABIA" BY EDWIN ARNOLD (D. 1904)

EIGHT

Jack Skinner was going to die. He was unconscious in ICU.
Machines kept him alive, but they wouldn't for long. He was
ninety-three years old; he'd had every chance that life gives any
of us. Now it was time for Jack to die.

They called me. I had left my card at the nurses' station.
"Call me," I had told them. "I'm Jack's priest. I will come at
any time." I knew Jack was in crisis, and he and I had become
happenstance buddies.

I will never forget the first time we met. I was new to St. Paul's, making the rounds, visiting those homebound parishioners who couldn't make it to church. Jack couldn't make it to church. I called him, and he said, "Come on over." I did.

Jack lived at Heron Point, Chestertown's more expensive transitional nursing facility. I knocked on Jack's door. Nothing. I knocked again. Still nothing. I banged. Twice. Finally, the door opened, and there stood Jack, still imposing at ninety-three. He must have been a large man once, for he was still over five ten', and solid. His white mustache framed his strong mouth and chin, and his eyes were keen.

But Jack couldn't hear. Not a thing. Which is why he didn't hear my knocking on the door. I deduced this immediately and compensated for his disability by shouting. I could hear Jack's hearing aid. It emitted a high-pitched whine most people would not be able to hear—and certainly not Jack. Unfortunately, I could.

As soon as I sat down in Jack's living room, Jack asked me, "Do you mind if I invite Mickey?"

"Well, no," I answered.

Mickey was Jack's girlfriend. Yes, Jack's girlfriend. She was also a member of St. Paul's and also nearly deaf. She lived in the apartment across the hall, so Jack banged loudly on Mickey's door and shouted even more loudly, "He's here. Come on."

Jack was forceful, gruff, and impatient. He still acted in the executive persona he had spent a lifetime cultivating. Mickey, also about ninety, walked into the room. Jack introduced her, and we sat down, Jack to my left and Mickey to my right.

"Tell me when you moved to the area," I started.

"What?" Jack answered.

"When did you move to Chestertown?" I asked more loudly, looking straight at Jack. He shook his head, so I looked to Mickey for help.

Mickey looked at Jack, and yelled at him: "What did he say?"

Like a volley out of reach, Jack yelled back over my head, "Don't know," then to me, "Say it again."

This time I yelled. "When did you move here?"

Jack's hearing aid whined its high-pitch complaint louder. He looked at Mickey again. This time they both understood me, so he shouted at her, "When was it? Ten years?" With that, they started yelling past me at each other. I might as well have been watching a tennis match. My head went left, then right, then left again. I wanted to join the conversation, but couldn't match their volume. I listened.

But as I listened, I learned some things about the two of them, this anything-but-sweet older couple. Mickey and Jack had both been married before, and they would have married each other. They couldn't, at least not without losing Social Security or pension or some other form of income. So they kept apartments across the hall from one another and cohabited. Married without a license. Later I learned in earnest, Mickey loved Jack, and Jack, Mickey. Not long after Jack died, Mickey had a stroke and moved into the Talbot Wing of Heron Point, the nursing facility, into a room by herself. The Talbot Wing is the last stop, like Hotel California; you check in, but you can't check out. Mickey hung Jack's portrait on her wall, and she complained bitterly of loneliness. Still her eyes would turn soft when I would mention Jack.*

Jack slowly lost the use of his legs because of poor circulation. When he could no longer walk, he moved into the Talbot Wing. Mickey would visit, but he also felt alone, waiting to die.

Two months later, Jack worsened, and he was sent to intensive care at the hospital. They hooked him to machines, but only to keep him alive until his children could get there. They

---

* Mickey died in the Fall of 2005.

never came. When the doctor finally decided to let him die, the nurses called me.

"Mr. Skinner is going to die," the nurse on the phone told me.

"When?" I asked.

"This morning. We're going to unhook him in about an hour."

"You've talked to his children?"

"Yes."

"Are they coming?"

"No."

"What about Mickey?" The nurse didn't know about Mickey. I called Mickey. Mickey had lost one husband, and couldn't deal with losing Jack. She did not want to be there.

Like Superman in the phone booth, I changed out of my T-shirt and into my clerical shirt—the dog collar, they call it, my *S*—and drove to the hospital. And I prayed. *Be with Jack; be present with him.*

In ICU, the nurse greeted me. "We've been waiting for you." I asked her how long it would take once they unhooked Jack. She wasn't sure, of course, but guessed a couple of hours.

The nurse unhooked Jack from the machines. When she left, I read the Anglican prayer, Commendation at the Time of Death, known among Catholics as Last Rites.

Depart, O Christian soul, out of this world;
In the Name of God the Father Almighty who created you;
In the name of Jesus Christ who redeemed you;
In the Name of the Holy Spirit who sanctifies you.
May your rest be this day in peace,
and your dwelling place in the Paradise of God.
(Book of Common Prayer, p. 464)

I sat down next to Jack. And I held his hand. I read a psalm. And I wondered at my own temptation to make death holier than life. Had Jack walked the psalms throughout his life? Should they be prominent at the moment of his death? I don't know, except that death can be intimate, like the psalms are intimate, and both seem holy.

And isn't death merely a caricature? It looks like a stalker, but prayer and psalms expose its darkness, its exaggeration, its threat? I exposed the stalker by reading the Forty-Second Psalm and prayed more, but more than anything else, I touched. I held Jack's hand, and when I got tired of holding his hand, I latched onto his forearm. I touched Jack skin to skin because I wanted Jack to know that he was not alone, he would not die alone.

Sometimes people tarry. They fight the dark night. Jack didn't tarry. He didn't fight. He died with breath suspended, as if he would breathe again—only he didn't. And I'm here to tell you: as soon as Jack died, that second, I felt his skin cool. His surface temperature dropped instantly, as if the soul imprisoned by his old body escaped, and with his soul, the warmth that is life escaped, too.

This is how I knew Laura was dead and not asleep when I found her on the morning of June 7. Her temperature wasn't right; her soul, like a hummingbird, had darted away.

Laura's gallbladder surgery was scheduled for three in the afternoon. Until that day, I did not know doctors performed day surgery in the late afternoon. Any procedure I'd ever had or taken Laura to started first thing in the morning, but not this one. Check-in was scheduled for three in the afternoon.

I worked that morning. I probably jogged, too. Laura never said it, but suspected I'd jog if the house was on fire. The kids were in school, but my mother, who was visiting—"Reenie" to Tate and Tilly—picked them up in my Volkswagen Passat.

I drove Laura in her Suburban. Getting Laura into the Suburban could be a chore, but today she managed fine. At only five-six, I felt diminutive driving that big white beast.

As I mentioned, I was always careful not to presume to act as Laura's priest. I was her husband, her friend, her companion, her sparring opponent. Lots of roles I played, but not priest—except for today, at 2:47 in the afternoon, as we sat in front of the Kent and Queen Anne's Hospital, waiting for one of their wheelchairs. I put the Suburban in park, started to open my door to walk around, when Laura stopped me.

"Pray for me," she pled. "Bless me. On my forehead."

Protestants don't always understand the physical language of prayer—that your body posture itself becomes prayer. Kneeling is prayer. Lying prostrate is prayer. It matters whether you close your eyes or bow your head. It matters whether you listen, and not just speak. Whether you tilt your head, your ear heavenward, and listen for the whisper of God. Gestures matter, too. Crossing yourself in the name of the Father, and of the Son, and of the Holy Spirit seals grace to your soul. Certainly not all gestures, not all postures, are prayer. Faith alone suffices—for those with perfect faith. Some of us don't have perfect faith, and the motions of the hand become the motions of the soul, drawing us inward and upward. Or to put it another way, posture facilitates faith, becomes its conduit.

I prayed simply, that day, for God to be with my beloved, and as she wanted, I anointed her using my thumb and the oil of her own forehead "in the name of the Father, and of the Son, and of the Holy Spirit. Amen." And I blessed her.

This was gallbladder surgery. Laparoscopic. Simple enough, and my only worry was Laura's RSD. It took advantage of every weakness, invading the body further with each new procedure designed to help. I was afraid that even gallbladder surgery would exacerbate her already intolerable pain, but I never suspected death.

But it was just a few minutes later, in the operating anteroom, waiting her turn, that Laura looked up at me and said simply, "I've had a good life." *I've had a good life.* Just like that.

I dismissed her with a wave of my heart. "You're going to be fine."

Don Rypka is a good friend and parishioner. In fact, I think he's a better friend to me than I am to him. He waited with me during Laura's surgery. We both read—I had a novel, and he read magazines. About six o'clock, the sky darkened, lightning shot across the sky, and thunder railed its battle cry. Ark-like rain fell. But we were in the waiting-room cocoon, impervious to the war of the gods and the fight that had begun for Laura's life.

The surgery ended, successfully, said Dr. O'Connor. Don went home to his wife, Marie, while I waited for Laura to awake from anesthesia. Finally, they released Laura. She was groggy, still asleep, which should have clued me in, and if that shouldn't have clued me in, the discharge instructions should have.

I sat reading my novel while the nurse read groggy Laura her discharge instructions. "You may resume taking your regular medications," the nurse told a Laura still quite out of it.

I looked up from my novel. "You're kidding. Are you sure? Do you realize what medicine she's on?" Laura took lots of medicine. She had to. Methadone. Duragesic patch. Effexor. And so on.

"That's what it says. That's what the doctor says."

"Okay," I said, assuming the doctor knew. But the doctor didn't know. He didn't know that the cocktail of surgery medicines mixed with Laura's regular regimen and weakened system would trigger arrhythmia and kill her. I should have said more. Instead, I took Laura home.

She scooted upstairs on her bottom, backward. Scooting was less painful and certainly easier than climbing stairs for a woman still woozy from general anesthesia. I helped her into bed.

"I want something to eat."

She had not eaten a regular meal that she did not throw back up since her first gallbladder attack, almost four weeks earlier, at Disney World. She craved substance.

"No," I answered. "Let me get you toast and ginger ale. To get you started easy."

"Okay. And bring me my medicine."

"Where is it?"

"In the cabinet. Top shelf. I need the key, too."

Laura kept her medicine in a pharmaceutical lockbox. Laura's cousin had lost a two-year-old son who died after finding her arthritis medicine in her purse while on vacation. Patients with arthritis cannot open childproof pill bottles. Hers was the old-style pill bottle, the kind they used to dispense drugs in before someone invented the childproof bottles. At home, Laura's cousin kept her medicine out of reach, but on vacation, she absentmindedly left her medicine in her purse, on her bed, where her son could and did find it. Laura refused to tempt either fate or our children and kept her medicine under lock and key. She was also careful about doses—she followed doctors' orders scrupulously.

Laura took one full dose of medicine when I returned with the toast. I left to check on the kids and talk to my mom. When I checked back on Laura and collected her dishes, she had fallen asleep. I tucked her in and kissed her good night. She fell further down into the bed, snug. I slept on that old feather sofa downstairs in the television room that night, as I did anytime Laura was in severe pain. Our bedroom was at the end of the upstairs hallway, past Tate's and Tilly's rooms.

I would like to tell you that I slept fitfully that night. That I had bad dreams, or that an angel shook to wake me. I didn't, and the angels stood perfectly still. I've had more than my fair share of sleepless nights since, but not that night. I slept peacefully. I fell into the couch and slept until I heard Mom shuffle through the living room on her way to make coffee in the kitchen.

I got up at 7:00 a.m. that June 7. Katie, the churchyard dog, and I fetched the newspaper from its box on the street. The sky was blue, and the weather was more spring than summer. A beautiful day at St. Peter's gate.

I took the paper and my prayer book to the screened porch with a mug of coffee, where I stayed until Tate and Tilly awoke. I had forgotten to tell them the night before not to bother their mother in the morning—that she would be tired from her surgery, and sore. As often as not they would run into our bedroom in the mornings to greet her. But on this day, some blessed instinct brought them down the stairs first, and not down the hall to their mother.

They opened the door to the porch where I sat; I turned around. "Morning," I said. Each in their turn said good morning. "Don't wake Momma. Let her sleep," I told them, first Tilly and then Tate. "See if Reenie will get you some breakfast."

I don't remember their eating breakfast. I don't remember my eating breakfast. All I remember is deciding that it was time to get Laura breakfast. I was supposed to offer the invocation at my kids' last-day school assembly, and it was almost time to leave. Mom had gone for a walk, and the kids were now watching television.

Death is a foreigner; it doesn't fit in. It doesn't belong. It is awkwardly obvious. Even though Laura's body was the same— the lines on her face, the color of her hair, her thin, feminine hands, none of it had changed—the foreigner who is death now occupied her body, Laura's soul having escaped. They used to call the living "the quick" because the flesh is quickened by the soul; it moves even when the body is imperceptibly still. When I walked into that room darkened by the shadow of absence, I knew immediately. I knew.

I looked at Laura, but she wasn't there. I felt bewildered, confused.

Seconds and minutes froze in place. With the agility one finds when walking underwater, I pushed at Laura. "Wake up," I commanded without authority. "Wake up, Laura." Her face didn't change its expression. Her eyelids didn't flutter. Her lips didn't crack to whisper. "Wake up," I commanded. The pitch of my voice raised. "Wake up, Laura. Wake up." My mind caught up with my senses, and I finally shouted as much as cried, "No! Nooo!"

Tate later reflected, "You cry like a baby." He had heard me cry out, but he didn't know why.

I phoned 911. The lady told me to give Laura mouth-to-mouth. How do you tell someone it's too late? So I tried, but Laura was long dead. "You don't understand," I answered. "She's dead," I moaned into the receiver.

I hung up when the woman promised to send help. But what next? I wanted to crawl into a ball and wish the budding nightmare gone, but with two children downstairs?

So as my first act of single parenthood, I wiped my face and blew my nose and came downstairs. Each step was lead. At the same time, Mom walked up the front walk, back from her walk.

"Mom. Laura is dead."

"What?"

"She died, Mom." She knew I meant it. My face was contorted and red, and my eyes revealed shock. "The ambulance is on its way. Take Tate and Tilly to the parish hall before they get here." She did. I have no idea what she told them. I have no idea what went through her mind, or her emotions. Did she recall her father's sudden and premature death, or my father's premature death? Was she confused, or was I clear? Did she hear my words, or did she hear my expression?

I went back upstairs. To make sure? I don't know that, either. Maybe. To be with Laura? I suppose, but she wasn't there, was she? She was gone. Her soul had escaped. But had it left the room? I could not be sure.

An older missionary couple befriended Laura and me during seminary. Rogers Beasley spent years as a medical missionary in India with Trink, his wife. They were retired now, living in an old white Victorian house on campus at Sewanee. Their warped floorboards sloped toward the fireplace, and in winter, they kept a fire burning constantly. The hearth's warmth reflected their own welcome to me, once a stranger and now a friend. I never knew their house to be empty; they were never alone. I will never forget Trink's statement right after Rogers's funeral: *"It wouldn't be so hard if it hadn't been so good."*

About a year into my seminary education, Rogers discovered that he had ALS, Lou Gehrig's disease. Lou Gehrig's disease is a horrible, debilitating, and terminal disease that attacks the muscles, knocking them out of commission one by one, until at last, the lungs can no longer suck air into the system. Victims die by suffocation, fully alert, because the disease does nothing to alter the mind.

Rogers was about to die. Trink called their son, Battle, and urged him to come. Battle was out of town, but his son, eight-year-old Chalmers, was due to fly into the Nashville airport later that day, returning from a trip to the beach.

Chalmers knew his grandfather was very sick, so he brought him a conch shell from the beach. Chalmers's mom, Amy, picked him up at the airport and told him plainly, "Grandpa's going to die. We're going to see him. You can give him the

71

shell." Then she added: "I hope we make it. But if we don't… if Grandpa has died before we get there, don't worry." Amy had a wonderful way of easing her son into the notion that his grandfather wouldn't be there much longer. "If he has just died, his spirit will still be in the room, and you can still give him the shell. But if it has been a while…well, we'll go out to the cross. Grandpa will be waiting for you there, and you can give it to him." Amy meant the simple cross in Abbo's Alley, a garden path that swathed through part of Sewanee, and behind Rogers's and Trink's house.

Rogers died right before Chalmers and Amy arrived. Chalmers grabbed his shell, walked straight to Grandpa's bed, held the shell up and out, and said, "Look, Grandpa! You can hear the ocean so loud!"

The faith of a child. I suppose it was that feeling, the sense that Laura was somehow, improbably, nearby. Maybe it was the feeling that her body was itself a portal to her, wherever she was. Maybe it was simply that her body was suddenly all that I had left. Whatever the reason, I waited upstairs for the Rock Hall Rescue Squad to arrive. I stumbled back to our bedroom, climbed into bed next to Laura, kissed her cheek, and sobbed. And again, I cried like a baby. I willed her to be there with me, to be able to say good-bye, to be able to tell her…anything. To be able to say, "You can hear the ocean so loud!"

But if the ocean roared, I didn't hear it, for Laura's soul left us early that June morning, before the sun rose. And like the water that carves caverns into a rocky shore, her escape carved a cavern into my heart. All you could hear was hollow and loud beating.

Paul says not to grieve like unbelievers, as those without hope. Paul never married, at least as far as we know, and the delicate and woven relationship of a husband to a wife, and of a wife to a husband, escapes him. He understands the nature of love in the form of its behavior, as in members of a church, one to another: "love suffers long, and doesn't notice when others do it wrong."

What Paul fails to appreciate is the organic union of spouses, that they are no longer two, but one, that they have become as conjoined twins. Love isn't just about feelings and emotions, or even commitment. It is, as I said, the nature of two people as trees planted so close together that, over the years, their trunks become as one—two trees, one trunk, one being.

When Laura died—that day, perhaps that moment, as I lay on the bed, waiting for the ambulance—I understood for perhaps the first time that marriage is about the union of two people. For, you see, a part of me was suddenly gone, amputated, severed, leaving only a fraction of my soul. It wasn't that Laura had died; it was that I had died. And that is a grief not moved like mere mountains by faith, despite Paul's hollow advice. That grief is pure pain. It isn't that our marriage was better than anyone else's, or we were happier—our marriage was tough stuff; we faced struggles just like most people—but we were together. Now we weren't together, suddenly and inexplicably.

Some people said it was harder for me because I was only forty-three years old. When you get older, you expect your spouse to die, they would say. But age doesn't matter when you consider the bifurcation, one violently split into two.

For a couple of months after Laura died, people would ask me the inevitable question—"How are you?"—outside of church on Sundays, as I greeted the parishioners with a smile and a hug. Each questioner was well-intentioned, but only a small club of parishioners understood the enormity of the question. "Fine," I would always answer. *Fine*, with upturned lips.

Those willing me to be fine would say, "Good," and go on their way, relieved that I was bucking up, sucking it in, forcing myself through the Valley of the Shadow.

But the members of this small club of parishioners who had themselves lost a spouse would look me in the eye and say simply, "I know." And I knew they knew. They knew.

They knew those dark and hollow caves of existence that wouldn't see light for months, if not years. They knew the pain of amputation and the physical therapy required to rehabilitate me.

And so as I lay there empty beside the shell of my spouse, my soul escaped with hers, I wondered whether she could still hear me, or where she'd gone, to Knoxville, to Kenesaw Avenue, or perhaps to Sewanee, to the cross on the cliff. I hoped she could hear me. I wanted her to know, *You can hear the ocean so loud.*

My days are few, O fail not,
with thine immortal power,
to hold me that I quail not
in death's most fearful hour;
that I may fight befriended,
and see in my last strife
to me thine arms extended
upon the cross of life.

"O SACRED HEAD, SORE WOUNDED" (PAUL GERHARDT),
TRANSLATED BY ROBERT SEYMOUR BRIDGES
(HYMNAL 168)

NINE

The fear of death is death.

July 4, 1958. My grandmother awoke before him. The first slice of orange light shot across the floor, leapt onto the corner of the bed, and settled into the chaise where she had laid her robe the night before. She shoveled feet into slippers and poked arms into her robe. The robe was pink silk. Nan loved pink and silk. She was careful; she didn't make a sound. It was a holiday, and he didn't have to work. She let him sleep and went to the kitchen.

The kitchen faced west, so it was still dark. Nan turned on the light and plugged in the chrome-and-black percolator. She had filled the coffeepot the night before. Her garden tennis-shoes were in the mudroom, by the back door. She put those shoes on her feet and walked to the mailbox. Through the trees, Nan now felt the sun's early warmth. The air was heavy, and she guessed today would be hot. The thermometer had registered over ninety degrees for two weeks now, and today would be no different. No, today would be hotter. But that was okay with Nan; she liked the summertime. So did Bob. And they were going to his brother's house for a picnic. She liked his family better than her own.

Back in the kitchen, Nan spread the paper on the table, grabbed her first cup of coffee, and read. She read the society page first, to find hers or her friends' names. She then read about President Eisenhower and the Soviet threat, the Fourth of July parade down Gay Street.

Nan didn't usually like early mornings. They reminded her of Linda Ann. And mornings were busy. She had to cook breakfast for Bob before her head cleared, before the coffee kicked in. But today was different. It was a holiday. The morning was hers; it was quiet. Peaceful.

When she finished her first cup, the phone rang. It was my mother. Mom wanted to check on Nan and tell her that she would be late to the picnic. Mom was pregnant with me, and I was kicking hard. My due date was still three months out—October 6, my father's birthday—but I was rambunctious.

Nan hung up the phone, and with her solitude now broken, walked to the stove to cook breakfast. Bob, my granddaddy, was a pork meat packer, so Nan fried bacon and eggs for him every morning. Nan fried the bacon a little too crisply and set it aside. She scrambled the eggs—her choice, not his. He liked fried eggs, but scrambling was easier.

She scrambled the eggs, and as she did so, she thought about her only living child, her daughter, with her two—and almost three—grandchildren. She adored those children, but she worried about them, too. She worried about Butch the most. Butch was the oldest, and he seemed to struggle to learn some of the basics. She was afraid for him. She was afraid because Paul, her son-in-law, didn't notice, or worse, he didn't seem to care.

It irritated Paul when Nan asked questions about Butch. But then, everything she said irritated Paul. It was none of her business, he had told Reenie. Butch was his child, not hers. But he was wrong. It was her business, especially now. Reenie was her only daughter, and Reenie's children were her only grandchildren. Nan had lost Linda Ann, her baby, five years earlier, when Linda Ann was ten. That was the year before Butch was born. Butch was her baby now. Nancy—her second grandchild, Butch's little sister—was, too. So how could Paul deny her that pleasure? But he seemed to think she was an interloper when she didn't tell, really, but hinted at how they should live their lives and raise their children.

The scrambled eggs were hot, so Nan walked back to the bedroom to wake Bob. The curtains were still drawn, and because the sun was a little higher, the room was actually darker than earlier. Nan couldn't see his face from the doorway, so she walked over to the bed and sat down beside him. She wondered at this man—he was a good man, this she knew. She had her hidden side, her dark side, but not Bob. Bob was exactly what you saw. He didn't hide things, and he was happy.

She reached her hand to his, to squeeze it, to wake him. At the same time, she looked into his face, and those dual senses, touch and sight, whispered into her ear, but their voices were too soft. She noticed that there was no movement, no stirring, no hint of dreaming on Bob's face. His hand felt rubbery to her touch. His tranquility was exaggerated and wrong, something deep inside of Nan told her.

She pushed at him. "Wake up, Bob. Breakfast is ready." Only she pushed a little too hard and spoke a little too loudly. He didn't move, again, and he didn't twitch. She pushed harder this time, nothing. *Nothing.* No, something, which is worse than nothing. His skin, she realized, was ghostly white, ashen, and her depressions on his skin did not reinflate. No, they did not reinflate, and the processes in her brain, its synapses, the electrical loop, closed, and current finally flowed, and she finally knew.

But she couldn't know. So she yelled, "Bob! Bob! Please, no, Bob!" Nan screamed. And she yelled it again. And again. And she grabbed his head from behind, and pulled it to her bosom, and begged, "Please, no. No. Not again. No." But there was no life in him. The blood had stopped its endless racetrack circulation, his heart had failed him, and it had failed her. He was only fifty-four. And so was she. Too young for two deaths. Too young to be a widow. Nan sobbed.

For ten minutes Nan sobbed. Next, she composed herself and picked up the phone to call not my mother, but Paul, my father. How could she tell my mother, who was so pregnant, that her daddy had died? She told my father, and for all their faults together, he came to her right away, and they faced this hell together.

When you find someone unexpectedly dead, it affects you. I know. I found Laura. I think I know what Nan felt. And I know what she felt later. What she felt later, during her second marriage, each morning when she awoke before he did, wondering to herself, but afraid to give voice to her thoughts: *When I go to kiss him, will he be alive?*

For months after Laura died, I would go into Tate's and Tilly's rooms after they were asleep to make sure they were still breathing. If I couldn't hear them, I would walk in, and more than once, I bent over them, my ear to their mouths, straining to hear, to make sure life had not escaped during the night. The fear of death.

I also remember the morning sweetness of waking them up. I would walk into their rooms, pull their shade, and just look at them. One day, after pulling the shade, I walked over to Tate's bed. He must have been deeper in sleep than usual at seven thirty in the morning, so I sat down beside him. He didn't stir, but he didn't have to. He didn't move. His eyelids didn't twitch. I couldn't hear his breath. It didn't matter. I could tell. I could sense only life in his still, little body. I reached behind his head, pulled it close to me, kissed his forehead, and said, "Good morning."

Tate's eyes opened. He looked up at me—Laura's eyes looking up at me—and he smiled, and said softly, "Good morning." Good, indeed.

Mary and Martha did not think Lazarus would die. They had sent envoys to Jesus. Jesus was their friend, their companion. They were there when he healed perhaps hundreds of people, so they knew he could, and would, heal their brother, his friend. They slept peacefully because Jesus would soon come. But Jesus didn't come; life did not come. Death came, and I wonder, was it in the middle of the night? Did Martha and Mary awake the next morning, surprised to find Lazarus replaced by a corpse? To find death as a dark dream occluding? And whoever found Lazarus early that morning would have done what is so human. Grab the body in your arms; rock her; kiss her head; and sob uncontrollably. You breathe near or into the body, as if your breath is life, as if it is all a mistake, as if she needs but a reminder to wake up, to live another day.

But you can't wake up the dead. That time has passed. Lazarus' time had passed, and Jesus knew it. "Lazarus is dead," he told his followers, maybe even before Martha and Mary knew. And it is, perhaps, Jesus' fault that Lazarus was dead, because he waited days before coming to Lazarus. If he had come when they called, he would have healed Lazarus. He didn't come. Lazarus died.

When Jesus finally showed up, Mary and Martha were angry: "If you had been here, our brother would not have died." But when Jesus saw Mary—no, not when he saw her, but when he sensed her—he wept. No, not wept, but shuddered with sadness.

The cruel grip of death on humanity angers this Messiah—it squeezes everyone tightly. Jesus *feels* this. He felt what Mary felt, he felt what Martha felt, he felt what Nan felt, and he felt what I felt. He feels death's crooked and jarring smile at us, its high-pitched laugh at the human race, that viceroy grip around our collective throat. Lazarus was asleep, not dead. We are dead. We are dead because death has gripped us. Has us in its clutch. We believe more in death than we believe in life, and death laughs wildly.

"Lazarus," Jesus said, "is asleep." Jesus believed this; but death itself did not believe Lazarus was asleep. Death believes it has won, and it knows that you believe it too, that I believe it, too.

Jesus shudders with grief. He sobs your sobs. He bears your fear; his body is wracked with it.

Neither Mary nor Martha could revive Lazarus. Neither Mary's nor Martha's breath could revive Lazarus, just as my breath on Laura's lips could not revive her. My breath was not Laura's breath; nor was it the breath of life.

The breath of life is God's breath. It is the *ruach* of God, the wind of God, that hovered over the deep at creation. This same breath is Elijah's still breeze. This wind blew from the corners to ignite dead souls attached as sinews to bones in Ezekiel's valley. There stood the bones, the flesh of Israel, when God breathed, and so did the bones.

But the *ruach* of God abandoned Jesus on the cross. God's life escaped Jesus' chest when he died, and all that was left was death. Death won the battle. Death eclipsed the sun, and the sky grew dark. The earth quaked, and people fled. The palpable terror at the cross was as on the last day, the day of judgment. The victory of nothingness.

Same, the *ruach* of God fled Granddaddy's and Laura's mortal bodies. Ashes to ashes, dust to dust. God's breath escaped just as it had from Lazarus, and there I was, with Mary and Martha, one in spirit. My senses dulled, and life, as a movie, projected in slow motion, demanding an answer, *If you had been here, she would not have died*.

Telling Tate and Tilly that their mother had died was the hardest and most painful moment of my life. After the rescue squad arrived, I walked over to the parish hall, into my office, where Mom waited with Tate and Tilly. Mom stood there while I told them.

The four of us returned to the house. I wanted to give Tate and Tilly the chance to say good-bye to Laura in person, to see her before the rescue squad took her away. And that's when Tilly said, "She's not dead. She's right there." How do you tell a five-year-old that the body is but casing?

Later that morning, someone took Tate and Tilly from me. Because children feel more acutely than we do, their systems shut down. They process death in bits, pieces at a time, and only as their system allows, so that afternoon, they were off to play with friends. I can't imagine what or how they felt.

I phoned Lewis, Laura's dad. How do you tell a man *his* baby girl died?

Perversely it was a bluebird day, not a cloud in the sky, eighty degrees. Laura and I had purchased a green lounge chair for the screened porch, a soft one that shapes to fit the body. We bought the chair for Laura, hoping she could sit in it without pain. I sat in Laura's chair the rest of the afternoon. I watched the birds at the feeder. As I sat and watched, it occurred to me that I'd never bought Laura the thistle seed she'd asked for. She wanted to watch goldfinches from that green chair, and from her spot on the couch in the living room.

My friend Mike Totten came by. Someone (who was it?) let him into the house and out to the porch to see me, as I sat there staring at the birds. And Mike asked me, "What can I do?"

I answered, "Go to Ace's Hardware and buy thistle."

Mike went to Ace's. He came back to the house with thistle and two heavy wrought-iron garden crooks to hold feeders. Mike stuck the crooks into the ground behind the screened porch, filled feeders with thistle, and hung them. For the next three days, I watched goldfinches, ochre females and the Crayola yellow, and I pondered absolutely nothing and absolutely everything. I pondered that the goldfinches live, and die, and continue to live, at that holy place on Maryland's Eastern Shore. That we live, and die, and continue to live there, too.

I watched goldfinches all that day, and I wrote Laura's obituary the next.[1] I refused to send her off with a morbid recitation

---

1   **Laura Howard Gieselmann,** of Kent County, died unexpectedly in her sleep on the morning of June 7, 2002. A gifted mother who deeply loved her children, Tate and Tilly, Laura created a happy and imaginative home for her family. Her fanciful, hand-painted murals decorated the walls of the childrens' rooms, and her creative touches offered a warm welcome to friends. She and Rob, her husband of ten years, enjoyed the unique adventure of love balanced by a sense of true friendship. And, from *West Side Story* selections to "Open Thou Mine Eyes," Laura would sing. As a young woman, she sang with the traveling troupe Up with People, and more recently, she sang to her children and for her church. Educated at

of her life. I wanted her to sound alive and human. I refused death its due. And so did Jesus.

Jesus looked into the tomb of Lazarus after they rolled the stone away. He called Lazarus, and Lazarus came out, bound hand and foot and with head in a death shroud. "Unbind him," Jesus commanded dumbfounded onlookers.

Death loses against the breath of life, the spoken word of God. And don't ever, ever forget that life is our hope and our faith and our belief. It is with life that we take our stand. Not with death.

It is not enough to comfort those of us whose life has been occluded by the canopy of death with the simple temporal promise that God never leaves us nor forsakes us, that God is with us now, even at this horrible moment, that God wants to hold our hand. I don't want to hold God's hand, thank you very much. I want to know that death hasn't won. That this god-awful and hopeless darkness that I face isn't eternal, and that I can hope in tomorrow, in an eternity of emerald and gold behind a bronze Oz door. That this very powerful Messiah is

---

the University of Tennessee with a double major in English and Spanish, Laura went on to become a Certified Public Accountant, practicing in both Knoxville and Sewanee, Tennessee.

In addition to her immediate family, Laura leaves behind her father, Lewis S. Howard; her siblings, Cathy Howard, Martha Howard Ayres, and Lewis S. Howard; her stepfather, Jack Hamilton; and her nieces and nephews, Emily, Meredith, Paige, Ellis, Morgan, Carrie, J.P., Christina, and Max. Sadly, Laura's mother, Anne Hamilton, died seventeen months ago.

Funeral services will be held at the Church of the Ascension, Knoxville, Tennessee, at 10:00 A.M., Thursday, June 13. A memorial service will be announced later and held at St. Paul's Episcopal Church, Chestertown, Maryland. In lieu of flowers, Rob, Tate, and Tilly have asked that donations be made in Laura's name to Episcopal Relief and Development, 815 Second Avenue, New York, NY 10017, or to Reflex Sympathetic Dystrophy Association, P. O. Box 502, Milford, CT 06460.

the One who, for all time, beat death at its game on the cross and at the tomb, the One who called Lazarus forth, and the One who, person by person, called Laura, calls your name, and then mine, and then the next person's.

"I am the resurrection and the life. He who comes to me will never die." Laura, whose forehead is crossed in the name of the Father, the Son, and the Holy Spirit with the oil of her own humanity is alive, though she has died. Not because of some ephemeral spiritual belief that our spirits rise and float around like mist, but because Jesus is alive. Three days. So is Laura. She is Alive. Not dead. Alive! How or why or where, I don't know. A shadow somewhere, awaiting a final day, or alive already in the world next door, I don't know. But because Jesus is alive, Laura is alive.

And Granddaddy, too, and now Nan, for she has since died. Plus, all of the dead in Christ, and who knows, perhaps the work of Christ, the work of life, will extend beyond mere Christianity and encompass all of creation—for wasn't that the goal in the first place, that through Christ the whole world might live, and not die?

So, isn't death's victory an illusion, its only grip being fear? The fact that we are afraid to die, and afraid when others die? We focus on death because we are afraid of death, or the opposite—we avoid the subject of death because we are likewise afraid of death? But our hope, our confidence, our faith is in life, in Christ. We can live because death is a passage and not the end. Paul is wrong when he advises not to grieve as others. We must grieve—but, we need not fear. We can live with confidence. Because of grace. Jesus at the grave, calling Lazarus's name, your name, my name, Laura's name. Come forth! Unbind her!

*Talk to me about the truth of religion and
I'll listen gladly.
Talk to me about the duty of religion, and
I'll listen submissively.
But don't come talking to me
about the consolations of religion or
I shall suspect that you don't understand.*

—CS Lewis

TEN

I think of heaven as a parallel universe, existing simultaneously with this world, side by side. Not up and down, sky and earth, but side by side. Or perhaps, one within the other.

Mr. Mxyzptlk was one of Superman's nemeses; at least he was in the 1960s when I was a boy. Mr. Mxyzptlk came from a fifth dimension to torment this world—by, for example, causing the rides at an amusement park to spin dangerously out of control. Mr. Mxyzptlk was shrewd and fast, and Superman could defeat him only by tricking him into saying his name backward. When he did, he was pulled instantaneously back into that fifth dimension. The barrier between the two worlds opened but for the briefest of seconds, as if by pinprick, and Mr. Mxyzptlk was sucked by vacuum into it.

Death is a pinprick in the fabric of this temporal universe, in the fabric that separates this world from heaven. At death, the soul is sucked, like Mr. Mxyzptlk, into the next world, and once the soul is through, the breach closes. The body left behind cools instantly, for the embers of the soul no longer warm it.

There is no elevator from this world to the next, no aboveground passageway as if from skyscraper to skyscraper. The only transporter is death.

I cannot help but wonder if the bright light people see through a tunnel at the end of life is the breach in the fabric separating dimensions—heaven as irrepressible light exploding through a tiny hole.

At the very moment Laura's mom, Anne, died, Laura was in the car with her sister Martha, driving from Tennessee to South Carolina one last time to see her, both trying to steal one last visit from death. They didn't make it. Anne died before they got there. Because Laura was not at home, I had the job of telling Tate and Tilly that Grandmomma had died. Tate was six; Tilly was three. We still lived in Cleveland (Tennessee).

I called Tate and Tilly into the living room. I put one on my right and the other on my left so each would be within hugging reach. They had heard that Grandmomma was going to die of her cancer—we had been to visit her at Christmas, and that was why we visited, to say good-bye. They knew this much, but did they understand?

Laura and I always shot straight with Tate and Tilly. Lying to children about death—even using euphemisms—is absurd. Kids know when you're lying or obfuscating, and then, on top of their grief, they feel betrayed.

So I told them plainly, "Grandmomma died today." We sat quietly, the three of us, if only for a minute. In retrospect,

I doubt Tilly could grasp death yet. I'm not sure she even remembered Grandmomma between visits.

Tate understood; he grasped the concept of death. "I know where Grandmomma is," he said, breaking the silence.

"Really?" Did I really want to know what he thought?

"She's a new star in the sky."

I thought maybe he'd picked up this concept from one of his books. I asked him, but he said no. He'd thought it up on his own. "She's a star," he continued, "because that way she will always be able to see me."

My friend Adrianne Burton, a retired nurse, recently told me about Mike. Mike was a boy dying of cancer. Adrianne and the entire staff of the pediatrics ward at the University of California Hospital in San Francisco wanted to tell Mike he was dying. He sensed it, they knew he sensed it, and it was a lie not to tell him. Mike asked them questions like, "Why am I not getting any better?", after enduring multiple treatments over long months to make him better. Each treatment failed, and his little body fagged. He knew something was terribly wrong, but nobody would tell him the truth. They didn't tell him because his mother wouldn't let them. For months he wondered; for months nobody would tell him the truth.

Mike's mother wanted to protect him, a mom's number one job. In her mind, she thought she had failed; Mike was going to die. If she couldn't protect him from death, she decided, she would protect him from the knowledge of death. She wanted to protect his hope. Nobody can blame her for that. "You can't tell him; you won't tell him," she warned.

Truth won't hide behind rocks, even for kids. Mike *got it*. When he would broach the subject of death with the medical staff, all they could do was shrug their shoulders. "It'll be all right, Mike." They would turn away; they didn't want Mike to see them cry.

One night, Mike asked his favorite nurse, Leal (pronounced "Layel"), "Wrap me in a blanket and take Mike and me outside. I want to go outside." "Mike" was the doll they had made for Mike that looked just like him. Mike became Mike's medium. He used Mike to tell the doctors and nurses how he was feeling.

Leal said, "No, Mike. It's too cold."

Mike persisted. "Please. I want to go outside. I need to go outside."

"Okay. But let's bundle you tightly." So Leal did bundle Mike and Mike tightly, and she carried them both to the roof.

After Mike settled into a chair Leal found for him, and they stared into the sky for a time, Mike finally asked Leal, "Do you see that star up there?"

"Which one?"

"The bright one." Maybe it was the North Star.

"Yes. I do."

"That star is my grandmother." She had died just a few months before.

Then Mike pointed to the right of the star. "Do you see the star right next to it?"

Leal didn't see that star and didn't know whether to humor him or tell him the truth. He asked her again, "Do you?"

Leal decided upon the truth. "No, I'm sorry, I don't."

"That's because it isn't there. Promise me something."

"What?" Leal couldn't tell where this was going and was worried.

"Promise me," he continued. "Tomorrow, will you come back out here and look up into the sky? You'll see it then. The star. You'll see it tomorrow night."

Mike died that night, at two in the morning. He intuited he was dying, and in his little mind, he was going to be a star, just like Tate knew his grandmomma was a star. Maybe the star children see and we don't is that pinprick into heaven as the universe next door. Light radiates as a tiny explosion from this other dimension, this parallel universe.

Because of Mike's intuition, Leal called his mother, who came in that night for what would become her good-bye, her last "I love you."

Who knows what children perceive? Romantic thoughts, sweet thoughts? The cycle of life?

But now, with Laura's death, there were no such romantic thoughts. Tate had lost his mother, he knew it, and he was angry. At barely five, Tilly didn't understand death, but she felt it. She felt the darkness, and she knew her mother was someplace else. These several years later, she is still wrestling with her very real loss. Every so often, she asks through tears, "Why did she have to go?"

Those who think children don't appreciate death are wrong. They appreciate it. They feel it, and they grieve, just like the rest of us, for the rest of their lives.

And so, Laura was translated into the world next door— heaven, the universe of light. Despite her unrelenting pain, she didn't want to go. Not yet. She wanted to live long enough to see Tate become a paleontologist, and Tilly a ballerina. She wanted to return to Australia, and she wanted to write her book. She wanted to sing in church again, and someday, she wanted to return to Tennessee.

She was pulled, against her will, through a tiny hole in the shroud veiling this dimension, the curtain severing this universe from the next, this shadow world from that of white light.

For days after I found Laura dead, life slowed. I walked as if underwater, as if slogging through a swamp of molasses. My arms and my legs had weights tied to them. Seconds became minutes, and minutes became hours. That day, after Laura left, literally after her body left the house, after I signed whatever it was I signed, after I offered a polite but out-of-place thank-you to the chief paramedic, after someone came and took the children away, I sat on the screened porch, in Laura's green lounge chair—as I said, the one we bought for her because it was soft and wouldn't poke her pain points—and I stared, as if into space. I wanted desperately to see through the veil and into the next world. So I stared. For hours.

That's when Mike Totten came by. Other people, too, Barbara and Frank Harriman, Pete and Pat Dillingham, Chris and Beverly Porteus, Bill and Kathleen Chilton, all dropped by to offer their condolences, to hold me tight. Edith Foley made a sandwich for me—or was it dinner? The Robinsons organized my life. Very few people spoke to me. What could they say?

And with that, just as Laura was pulled against her will through some pinprick in eternity, I was sucked into some bizarre mirror universe. Mine was the Old Testament *Sheol*, the land of the dead, a place of half life, a shadow life, only my heart still beat in this shadow world. In this shadow world I lived for weeks, and months, and even years, and although the light of day grew brighter over time, the shadows are still long because—no matter what they say—there is no straight path leading you out of the valley of that shadow. That shadow world became home to me, just as it has to anybody who loses a partner. Partners without partners understand; partners with don't.

It is shock, they say. Paralysis. Numbness. Your system protects itself, contracts, and finally, shuts down.

My brother Pete, who was a housepainter at the time, stopped painting whatever house he was painting, hopped in his car, and drove four hours to me. I don't know what thoughts crossed his mind as he drove. Death was rare in those days, it seemed; how was he going to handle me? What would he say? In the end, he didn't say anything. He just came.

So did Jamie and Eleanor Stutler. Jamie and Eleanor lived in Kingstree, South Carolina, then, and were friends from seminary. Best friends, really. Eleanor, in tears that her best buddy Laura had died, met me at my kitchen door with the biggest hug, after she and Jamie drove eleven hours. That day. They stayed with the Dillinghams, who treated them like family.

That night, when Tate and Tilly came home from wherever it was they had been—Matti Meehan took them to play with her kids, I think (didn't Shirley Nicholson help somehow?)—we crawled into bed together, into Laura's and my bed, the death-bed. I refused to let that four-poster bed that was our marriage bed, and a bed of life that Tate and Tilly had climbed onto from the time they were toddlers, become a bed of death, so out of force of will, we climbed into it together and tossed and turned and slept not much at all that night. I didn't want Tate and Tilly to become afraid of sleep; that's why we slept together. I didn't want Tate and Tilly to become afraid of death; that's why we slept together. I didn't want to become afraid of death; that's why we slept together. Someone must have washed the sheets and made the bed for us that day, but I don't know who.

Laura's first funeral was in Knoxville, two miles from Kenesaw Avenue, at our home church, the Church of the Ascension.

I am Resurrection and I am Life, says the Lord.
Whoever has faith in me shall have life,
even though she die.
And everyone who has life,
and has committed herself to me in faith,
shall not die for ever.

As for me, I know that my Redeemer lives
and that at the last he will stand upon the earth.
After my awaking, he will raise me up;
and in my body I shall see God.
I myself shall see, and my eyes behold him
who is my friend and not a stranger.

Julie sang her lonely solo, and Bishop Tharp told the story of our first dinner together, Laura and Bishop Tharp, Bill and Margaret Squire, Margaret Mullen and me, when Laura, so much like her mother, spied uneaten spinach and greens and pecans and pears on Bishop Tharp's salad plate at Pearl's Cafe outside of Sewanee and asked, "Are you going to finish that?"

He smiled ever so kindly and said that no, he wasn't, and did she want half, as though people you just met ask every day whether you are going to finish everything on your plate. Bishop Tharp died about two years later, of cancer. Another one of my heroes gone.

During the funeral, with so many people around us, as Julie sang, as Bishop Tharp spoke, Tate reached up to my cheek with his hand, his little fingers bent, and wiped away my tears. Eight years old.

The church had an anteroom where we waited for family to arrive. My immediate family came—all except Pete, who came to the second funeral—including my father's brother Kent and his wife, Kathie, from Memphis. Laura's family came, too. Lewis, Laura's dad, was there. He looked strained, thinner, older somehow, as you do when your baby dies.

After the reception during which I cried in the arms of hundreds, we went to Lewis's house, the brick Georgian on Kenesaw Avenue, where friends came by, and we loosened ties or collars (in my case) and laughed a little, gossiped a little. The best eulogies seem to be offered at receptions and homes when families and friends gather, not at services. We eulogized Laura that afternoon. We remembered the real Laura.

St. Paul's held a memorial service later, on July 3, almost a month after Laura died. The summer air hung humid and heavy at one hundred degrees. Pete brought his family to be with us, and his two children, JP and Christina, Tate's and Tilly's ages, played outside on the Slip 'N Slide before the service with Tate and Tilly. They slipped and slid up and down the canary-yellow vinyl sheet, with headstones to the right and to the left, not more than twenty-five feet away.

While we were getting ready for the four o'clock service, the electric grid in all of Kent County shut down, and with it, the church's air-conditioning. We held the service anyway, and Bishop Charles Longest, a man who understands grief from the loss of his son earlier in his own life, led us. Because the air-conditioning was off, it was probably 110 degrees in that little country church packed with friends and parishioners, but I wasn't about to take my coat off. Laura died; the least I could do was suffer a little heat. So I sweat, and so did everyone else, because no one would take off their coats unless I did. I briefly worried about the ninety-year-old men in the room, but considering them was more than I could handle.

I didn't preach for two months after Laura died, and then only every other week. I celebrated the Eucharist about a month after, but preaching is intimate. I couldn't expose myself so carelessly. I needed more space, more time. Friends and colleagues and friends of friends helped out.

That summer and fall, all of life was tilted, skewed, out of sorts. It was a dark and cold winter that attached itself to me, persisting until Christmas. Christmas was hard, as anyone who has lost someone close will tell you, but our anniversary was the hardest. On December 19, I drove myself to a restaurant to re-member—by myself—ate a filet mignon, talked to a Laura who wasn't there, and then, when I got in my car, everything inside of me exploded. All of these months of winter became at last too much, and there, in the parking lot of the restaurant, out of view, and yet in view of anyone walking by, I sobbed. And when I finished sobbing, I drove to the shore of the Chesapeake, and looked across the bay to Baltimore, and sensed a loneliness I've seldom felt. Not a loneliness of being alone, or by oneself, but a loneliness of being subdivided from oneself. That loneliness is the worst of all, and that is what I felt.

Christmas came and went, and so did the New Year. The low-lying winter cloud cover lifted just a bit; the sky became steel gray, less threatening. It stayed steel gray for a long time. The clouds hid God from view, and I wondered at it all. I also jogged through it all—ran, really—as one runs from or to some-thing. My pace became my spirituality, the rhythm of footfall on Ricauds Branch Road, with no cars and no people, only me with God, with rhythm. Day after day, week after week, year after year. God I found not in my emotions or in my thoughts but in my solitude—a gift of solitude that was not loneliness, but being alone. Otherwise, it seems, God hid from me, and perhaps I from God.

But the odd miracle through all of this is Tate and Tilly, and the simple fact that the three of us drew closer, and not more distant, because of Laura's death. Her death was hard in its way for each of us, but our souls were raw and scraped and bloody in a way few could understand. We were vulnerable, if only to each other. Now, we are closer. Like Jacob who wrestled the angel, we will walk with a limp the rest of our lives, but if you watch all three of us, we limp alike.

So it is with death and new stars and Sheol. Worlds of parallel and mirror universes, a thick winter of darkness yielding cautiously to life and light as pinpricks in fabric that illuminate our world. Laura, perhaps, is the star to the right of her mother. You can see her if you look through the glasses of your imagination.

"When you wish upon a star, makes no difference who you are, anything your heart desires, will come to you..." (Jiminy Cricket)

Not too quickly now. Don't invoke resurrection prematurely. Resurrection takes God-awful time. Real time elapses after real death. Whitewashing tombs with quick drying Easter colors is merely putting makeup on a corpse. Real resurrection only comes after real death.

—WILLIAM SWING

ELEVEN

December 2002

Dear Family and Friends,

Christmas is near, and I am wondering what to write that might sound Christmas-y. It feels like Christmas, but I don't feel like Christmas. Tate, Tilly, and I are still struggling to make sense of this senseless year (a sentiment I suspect God of echoing). If Laura were in my shoes, she would have faced the Christmas challenge by writing one of her witty Christmas letters—you remember, the letters with humor that cut to the edge. I don't have Laura's gift, but I wanted to write to you anyway.

The truth is, I must write to you. I want you to know how much your prayers have meant. How much your letters and calls have meant. How much your visits, or plans to visit, have meant. I have discovered what most of us have long suspected, that a large part of life's meaning is hidden in the oak beams of support that are our friends and family. So many of you came to Laura's memorial services. Others sent flowers or made donations to the RSDS Foundation, to St. Paul's Church, St. Luke's Church, Episcopal Relief and Development, Rachel's Lament, or someplace else. Thank you. I wanted to write personal thank-yous, but every time I started, I shoved the task aside. It was just too hard—so let me say now, *thank you*, to each of you.

When Laura, Tate, Tilly, and I moved to Maryland, Laura promised to decorate Tilly's room with fairies, to paint a mural on her wall, just like she had done for Tate when he was born. Some of you may remember the huge *cow jumping over the moon* on one wall, with a little laughing dog and dish running away with a spoon on the opposing wall. For some reason, Laura didn't paint Tilly's room right away. Maybe she was occupied with unpacking. Maybe her RSD pain was too severe to let her stand for the long hours required. Whatever her reason for delaying, Laura decided in late May that it was time to paint, so paint she did. And she continued painting. Long hours and daily. I criticized her: *Settle down. You don't need to finish yesterday. The wall isn't going anywhere.* No, the wall wasn't going anywhere, but who could know?

Laura finished the mural on Tilly's birthday, and only three days later, she died. Before she went into surgery, she looked at me weakly and said, "You know, I've had a good life." I've had a good life. There. Like Jesus, *it is finished*. I blew her off: "Don't be silly." How could she know? How could she know what finishing a mural would mean to a little girl who still carries her mom's picture around with her, hoping…

Snow covers the ground today. Lots of it. I am sitting in Laura's seat on the couch, looking out the rectory's sliding glass doors. The back lawn slopes gently downward to the pond. The geese are walking on the pond, not swimming, because the pond has started to freeze. The songbirds stopped visiting the feeders a couple of weeks ago because I forgot to fill them. This was Laura's view, where she would wait out the pain. I am trying to imagine her, staring for hours at the birds, willing herself to outlast RSD pain, and the dark irony is that I'm doing the same thing: sitting in her seat, staring out into the back—trying to outlast the pain. They say you can outlast the pain; just be patient.

So, Tate, Tilly, and I are being patient. We are lucky to be in such a holy place, with a kind and friendly church family, and we are, believe it or not, looking forward to Christmas. Tilly asked me just the other day, "Will Santa really know where we live?" We plan to light candles for Laura on Christmas Eve, and that will be hard. But, we also plan to open more than our share of presents, enjoy the circus called the St. Paul's Christmas Eve children's service, and eat lots of turkey. And then, most of all, we hope to hear from you. For you are our life, and our oak beams of support.

Peace. Rob, Tate, and Tilly Gieselmann

The Epitaph
Here rests his head upon the lap of Earth
A Youth, to Fortune and to Fame unknown.
Fair Science frown'd not on his humble birth,
And Melancholy mark'd him for her own.

Large was his bounty, and his soul sincere,
Heav'n did a recompense as largely send:
He gave to Mis'ry all he had, a tear,
He gain'd from Heav'n ('twas all he wish'd) a friend.

No farther seek his merits to disclose,
Or draw his frailties from their dread abode,
(There they alike in trembling hope repose,)
The bosom of his Father and his God.

FROM "ELEGY WRITTEN IN A COUNTRY CHURCHYARD" BY
THOMAS GRAY

TWELVE

It had seemed forever since he'd played with another boy. It wasn't forever, only twenty-three years. Other boys had been buried here, at St. Paul's, but they had left—moved on. He couldn't be sure where they went, but he supposed it was to heaven. Why hadn't he? Twenty-three years gave him time to think, and thinking told him he'd died out of turn. Heaven or wherever wasn't ready for him, and here he was, dead. Twenty-three years.

He liked this churchyard home perhaps most for its hiding places. Hundred-year-old boxwoods formed canopies and tunnels and tents across the twenty acres, places he could hide. Places he could use to spy on others. He liked to spy.

He spied on funerals. Funerals were television for the boy— at least for a boy for whom there was no television. And funerals always offered something interesting. Like a twenty-one-gun salute. Or taps that he thought reminded him of water falling over rocks, from the end of the trumpet to the ground. Sound would run ankle-deep across the churchyard. He would dodge the water like children at the beach, but it would always reach him in the end.

He didn't like the funerals of other children. With the wailing and the carrying on. Didn't they know that their children were going somewhere good, he wondered. Isn't heaven somewhere good? Yes, it must be, he decided. When he was dying, his mom told him heaven was good. He would be okay, she said. And he was okay, even if this wasn't heaven. Not yet, anyway.

Dogs came to the funerals. *"Big dogs. Little dogs. Black and White dogs. Do you like my hat? I like that hat, I like that party hat."** The boy remembered this story from when he was learning to read. He remembered the big dog party at the top of the tree, and sometimes he would stare up into the old St. Paul's swamp oak, that 450-year witness to all who had passed through this particular place, and imagined the dogs up top, playing tennis and badminton and having fun. The boy would go to the top of the old tree sometimes, just to see if the dogs were there, but of course they weren't. Until recently, there

---

* P. D. Eastman, *Go, Dog. Go!* (New York: Random House, Inc., 1989)

weren't any dogs at all at St. Paul's, except for those who came to funerals, or those who would drop by for an hour or two.

The boy liked dogs. His dog was named, Ruthie, and after he died, his mom would bring Ruthie to his grave, and Ruthie, he was sure, could see him. She would bark as at nothing, as at him, and roll, and scratch her back on his grassy grave. He would try to pet her, but he couldn't. She knew when he tried, though, and she would bark again.

After a time, when his mom stopped coming every Sunday, Ruthie stopped coming altogether. Ruthie must have died, he wondered, but could not ask.

A while back, a family moved into the house on the property. The family had a dog. They called her Katie, and Katie spent lots of time with the boy. He supposed, to others, it looked as though Katie was wandering down to the pond to bark at the geese, or running off into the newer cemetery section to take care of business, but most often, Katie played with him when he was going to the pond to skip stones or into the new section to play hide-and-seek. He would climb the crooked cypress, the one split in the center about two feet up from the ground, forming a bench in a broad "y". Katie would watch the boy, and though they couldn't talk to each other, Katie was the only one who, he thought, understood him. Who knew he still existed—at least knew for sure. On the now-rare days when his mom came, she would talk to him, but she would talk to him as someone far off, not as he was, standing right next to her. Sometimes she would cry, and he would reach out to dry her tears, to tell her not to cry, to tell her he was okay—but she took his touch as a fly and swooshed him away.

Not long after the family moved into the house, he watched the boy and the girl, little kids, play outside. Sometimes they played outside without being coaxed, and sometimes their mom or dad made them. They would grumble for a while, but once they started climbing on the swing set, or playing tag, or riding their bikes, they would stop grumbling, and, well, the boy could tell—they were having fun.

Once in a while, the boy and the girl invited a friend to play with them, Julia. Julia and Tate, the boy, and Tilly, the girl, wandered through the churchyard together, their only restrictions being not to play near the pond, and not to climb on the headstones. Mostly they obeyed these simple rules, except for Tilly, who sometimes forgot and wandered too close to the pond, and Tate, who would get carried away with his sword fight and jump up on a tombstone. The stones never crumbled or broke, but one did fall over. Tate never told his parents about this so he wouldn't get into trouble. The boy saw all of this, but couldn't say anything—not that he would have, the code of kids and all.

Julia taught Tate and Tilly how to explore the churchyard, how to find its nooks and crannies, and together the three of them discovered the boy's hiding places, the boxwood tunnels and mazes. These became their hiding places, too, their secret ports of call. They also liked hiding behind the old swamp oak, but only on Sunday afternoons, so they, too, could spy on men and women who came to remember.

Katie would run and bark and hide with Tate, Tilly, and Julia, and even though he couldn't be heard by the others, or seen by the others (save Katie), the boy played with them, as well. He was older, he knew, and if he were still alive, would have been embarrassed to be seen with these little kids—but wasn't he still a little kid? Hadn't he died halfway between boyhood and manhood? He couldn't really translate those thoughts into words, but that's what he felt. So the boy liked it when Tate and Tilly and Julia would play together. He became their playmate; he became, wisping in and out of the boxwood like a breeze, essentially perceptible to anyone who might stop to pay attention. No one ever did. Except Katie.

It was a fine June morning when the boy heard the scream above the other June sounds. Above the birds' chirping, above the slight breeze in the trees and the distant cars. The scream split the day into two, and there was suddenly a before and an after. The boy stopped short when he heard the scream, for he recognized the sound, the sound of shock and unanticipated grief, only this time it was a man's voice. The last time he had heard that scream, it had been his mom's voice, but not this time. And to think, he'd been in this churchyard for these twenty-three years now. He'd seen death as a daily event, but never once had he been so near a sharp cry like his mom's, so near someone when they actually did the dying.

The boy floated across the chasm between his hiding place (nobody knows where it is, even still) and the house where Tate and Tilly lived, and he floated into the front door and up the stairs, and there in the bedroom, where he still heard the sharp notes of a man crying, he found them, together, one haunting the other, she having died just as the boy had died, and now having left her body. And in that surreal moment, the boy, as if yesterday, recalled his own mother gathering his empty body like a bag of dough into her arms to squeeze him and smother him, as if that were possible. But it wasn't possible, and it isn't possible for this man to smother this woman, and only for the briefest of seconds, this boy saw the woman who once occupied the body the man held, and she smiled at him as if she knew him, but she didn't know him. She smiled that knowing smile that all was well with her despite the chaos immediately below her, that all was well because her body is no longer a burden to her, binding her to Earth and pain. The boy saw this as a witness, and he wanted to tell the man that everything was okay, when the woman disappeared from the two of them, the man and the ghost boy.

He tried to tell the man that he had seen the man's wife. He swirled around the room, and around the man's head, and the man, like his mother, had swooshed him away like a fly, and he tried harder. He flew as a breeze might; they were inside, and not outside, and it should have worked, the boy thought, but it didn't work because the man was preoccupied and couldn't notice the breeze that didn't belong in a room with closed windows. People came to take her away, but didn't they know? She was already gone. He wanted to tell him, but he couldn't.

So the boy decided. He decided that he would tell his friends. He would tell Tate and Tilly that their mother was okay, but he couldn't tell them that day, because someone took them away. Three days later they went on a trip. When they returned, they didn't play in the churchyard; they were sad and didn't feel like it, he guessed. Just like his mom was sad those days after he died, when she came to his grave to remember. So instead of telling them, he waited for them to play outside again, and they did play outside again, and he played with them. And every time they played, he played. For three years, he played with them, darting to and fro throughout the churchyard, pulling them in this direction, and then that, and showing them the rest of his hiding places, the ones they hadn't yet discovered, and letting them share those hiding places with their new friends, with Charlie and then Isabell, and then James, and Natasha and Thad. And because the boy was only eleven when he died, and they grew older while he stayed eleven, they grew closer in age, and closer as friends. And when Tate and Tilly were sad or mad or unsettled because they didn't have a mom anymore, he would sit with them or cry with them or shout with them. He would hide with them in the boxwood maze, or crawl with them underneath. And while he never was able to tell them that he saw their mother smile, he knew that his friendship became to them a hope. He didn't know why, or how, but it was true.

It was so true that when Tate and Tilly moved, they felt a sadness they couldn't identify. It was as though losing a friend, someone you know you'll never see again. They knew they'd see Julia, Charlie, and Isabell, and James and Natasha and Thad and Sam again. But something deep inside told them that they were losing someone else, only they couldn't imagine who, and they didn't say anything to anyone else about that feeling. Not even to their dad.

And that boy, that breeze and breath of wind, that eleven-year-old messenger of God, also moved when they moved, for his time came at last to leave the churchyard. He waved at them as they drove off, and—he saw it—the girl, Tilly, turned to him as if she saw him, as if she'd seen him all along, and she waved back. While she waved, he smiled the smile of peace and disappeared just as the woman had disappeared before him. And for the first time in twenty-three years, the churchyard was completely empty.

*Death ain't nothing…Death ain't nothing but a
fastball on the outside corner…You get one of them
fastballs, about waist high, over the outside corner
of the plate where you can get the meat of that bat
on it…and good god! You can kiss it good-bye.*

—August Wilson

THIRTEEN

Sam was afraid of dying. Sam didn't attend church, but that is
not why he was afraid. He believed in God; he believed also in
Jesus.

Sam's wife, Lily, came to church almost every week. I met
Sam through Lily. Lily and Sam lived at Heron Point, in the left
side of a stand-alone duplex, with two bedrooms and their old
grandfather clock. A small patio looked out over grass.

Sam was a recovering alcoholic, sober for twenty-something
years. His sobriety made Sam one of my heroes.

Sam could not walk and lived in his wheelchair. He was
also completely deaf. Sometimes people treat deaf people as
they treat foreigners, as though they are stupid just because
they can't understand them. Sam was anything but stupid. He
spent his career as a psychologist, and he was a well-educated
and sophisticated thinker.

Because he did not sign or read lips, Sam felt isolated. He used an electronic amplifier with an earplug that barely helped. The first time I saw Sam with his amplifier, I thought of those old guys from a century ago with big horns held to their ears, yelling, "Whah? Whah? Wha'd ya say?" Sam, you see, would hold up his amplifier and yell, "Whah? Whah?" When his amplifier was working and when you talked directly into it, he could hear you, barely.

Sam asked many questions at the end of his life. Mostly, he wanted to know why *bad things happen to good people*, in particular to him. He felt like Job, wrestling with the spirituality of poverty, of physical poverty, and ultimately of death—that ultimately, we are in God's hands at the end, and will God be just?

Sam wanted to make sense of his own horrific end to life, and the fact that debilitation was a devil who had possessed his body and stripped him of his essence. I'm not sure I helped Sam much, but he persisted.

When I would visit Sam, I would stay only as long as he wanted. Sam always had a list of questions to ask me, and he would ask them—one by one by one—and when he was finished, he'd dismiss me: "That's enough, Rob. Thanks for coming." I appreciated his candor. I didn't have to read his mind or his body language, didn't have to intuit his secret thoughts (such as, *I wish this guy would leave. He's such a pest.*).

Sam became my friend. I suppose he became my friend because he engaged in honest struggle, with honest questions, and touched freedom in a way few people do—the freedom to think.

I think it was late 2004 when Sam took a bad turn and it became his time to move into the Heron Point Talbot Wing. He shared a room with another one of my parishioners, Charlie

Morrison. Both men bunked together until they died, each within several weeks of the other.

The room was a dirty pastel pink, and I wondered to myself, *Who put these two men in an ugly pink room?* The wood laminate industrial door opened into the room at its center, and Sam lay to the right, and Charlie to the left. The heads of the beds were against opposing walls. Each bed had a small window next to it, along the far wall. The hospital-like windows looked out over Heron Point's latest construction site. The beds were single hospital beds that you could raise or lower with buttons. Neither men could push the buttons.

I visited Sam every week or two while he shared that room with Charlie, but it was hard to have a good conversation with Sam when Charlie was both there and awake. It is hard to yell at someone when someone else is present. One day, Charlie took a bad turn and was sent to the hospital. That's when Sam and I talked. Sam was in deep physical pain, but the doctors didn't know why. He called it gout.

"Sam." I leaned over Sam, bent at my waist, and shouted again, even louder. "Sam!"

He was asleep without his electronic horn, so he couldn't hear me. I touched his shoulder, pushed at him just a little. I didn't want to push too hard and exacerbate his pain. Sam felt my hand and opened his eyes. Waking up, he felt his pain and knew he was still alive. He castigated me with his eyes; I should have left him asleep.

I told him as much, but he shook his head. "No." I shouted I'd leave, but again he said, "No. I want you to stay." So I stayed, to keep him company, but Sam, in Sam fashion, wanted to talk. He had his checklist ready. He must have been dreaming his checklist.

"I want to play the piano, again," he told me.

I didn't know Sam could play the piano, and I could tell by the way Sam said this, he meant *really* play—not pop tunes, but Rachmaninoff, Beethoven. He wanted the keys to absorb him, the reverberations to enfold him, to watch his fingers float above the keys. Play the piano again, but he couldn't play the piano again, because his fingers were bent with arthritis and he was in pain.

"What do you mean?"

"All I want is to play the piano one more time." *Before I die.* As I mentioned, Sam wanted to know why bad things happen to good people. Why this pain disease had happened to him. The question made Sam afraid, afraid of dying. *I'm afraid of dying*, Sam was trying to tell me.

But he was dying in increments anyway, one day at a time. He died the day he stopped walking, the day he stopped hearing, the day he stopped playing the piano. Death was Goliath, and Sam was afraid.

You're not the only one, I wanted to tell Sam. The world is full of people afraid—afraid of their shadows, of tomorrow, of the unknown, of being poor or alone, of growing old, of losing their jobs or security or family. People are afraid of war, and of terrorists. Of car accidents and drunk drivers. Of losing the people they love—even those people they don't love. People are afraid of losing the person abusing them. People are just plain afraid. *You're in good company, Sam.*

I didn't tell Sam he was in good company. I don't remember what I told Sam. I hope I let him vent, but I probably tried to fix him. *Trust. God is good, and God won't abandon you, now or at the time of your death. Trust that God will lead you safely home. God is trustworthy. I've seen that light, and it is bright. Trust.* I believed that—that the shortest route to control is through loss of control, through trust. But sometimes fixing a person isn't right; sometimes you just listen.

After a few minutes, Sam turned away. A tear escaped his eye and trailed onto his cheek, the stress too much for his worn-out-body. Sam was dying; he knew it; and he just could not face it. He just could not control death.

It was a week or two before I visited Sam again. He lay in the same bed, asleep. I shouted again. "Sam!" By this time Charlie Morrison had died, so Sam was still alone in the room.

He opened his eyes—gently this time, not hard as before. He looked up at me and smiled. I thought maybe he didn't recognize me. "It's Rob, Sam."

Sam stared at me, smiled peculiarly, then waved me down, into his face. I was tentative—why, I wondered. But slowly, I moved my face closer to his, thinking he might want to tell me something important, ask me some question. Now I was just a foot away, still close enough. Sam waved me closer with both of his hands, little circles in the air. I was uncomfortably in his space; he was in mine. He continued to wave me down, and reluctantly, I continued to edge down. Sam grabbed my face with his hands, took each cheek, and with his bent fingers he pulled me to within inches of his face. I became Elijah, my face on the dead boy's face, eyes to eyes, nose to nose, lips to lips. Sam kissed me, not on the lips, but on the edge, between my cheek and lips. He kissed me.

My chest exploded. I didn't know what to do, what to make of the kiss. I started, and then I pulled my face back. I looked down at Sam, now a foot away, and he smiled up at me, satisfied—but not satisfied, because he waved me back down. I wanted to walk out the door, but I didn't. I leaned down again, and he pulled my face once again, eyes to eyes, nose to nose, and lips to lips, and he kissed me again.

The kiss was not erotic, although at first I could not be sure. Later, I realized it was the deep kiss of a friend, a friend resurrected, but in the moment, I grew afraid. Sam violated every rule of protocol and decorum, and I was undone. Why had Sam kissed me? Did Sam lose his mind, literally? I wondered. No, he did not. He smiled the odd smile of love at me. Miserable Sam was suddenly happy. No, not happy, but unburdened.

I had nothing left to say, so I smiled back and left the room, pondering, befuddled. Contemplating the former bitterness, and this new joy.

It was not until later, after Sam died, that I understood. Sometime between my two visits, Sam had surrendered. He gave up control, and now, at last, he was at peace. Sam had crossed the threshold of fear, broken death's vise grip. He had seen the bright light *before* dying, heard angels' trumpets. Pure and simple, Sam beat death; he won, and he wanted to tell me. He didn't know how to tell me, so he kissed me. Sam's victory kiss. Death was no longer an event to Sam. The hell of fear was conquered, and God became resurrected for Sam, no longer the warden, suddenly the liberator. Freedom. Sam found his eternity in freedom, not in a prolonged existence.

I wanted to end all of this—death, Laura, grief—with a resurrection story, mine, about my own breakthrough, from grief to joy, from a stalled life to getting things revved again. About the second phase of my life. I read *The Life of Pi* several years ago, and when Pi boarded the steamliner, I imagined myself as Pi going to far and exciting places, recovering my sense of self.

Exotic places became mythical, and I became Pi, in a lifeboat, death, as sharks, encircling me. Sam's death was only one of dozens that I experienced after Laura's, often firsthand. I suffered death again and again and again. I performed funeral after funeral at St. Paul's, all the while needing the steamliner to take me to some distant shore, to be shod of the death's cloak.

Those encountering death are changed by it. I still suffer Laura's death—and Sam's, and Mike's, and Walt's, and Frank's, and John's, and Alfrida's, and Daddy's, and Nan's, and Mim's, and Granddad's, and Wilson's. I still suffer death, yet I have found a deep spirituality in the solitude of death, and know that I have touched God somehow in a deeper way, in a purer way, than before. My suffering has become a spiritual lifeblood. I *see* in ways I did not see before.

I'm not on Pi's steamliner. I'm on my own little rowboat, and I'm rowing desperately to some distant shore—a shore that is perhaps no farther than a hundred feet away.

As I said already, marriage does not end at the death of one partner—it ends at the death of both. I may marry again, but Laura will always be a part of me. So will my next wife. Death is not as simple as closing one chapter and starting another. You cannot turn the ship around, head for new destinations, begin again. You move ahead not only by demanding a life that is new and fresh, but by acquiescing, by trusting, by believing that God is good. "God is good. All the time. All the time. God is good."

Sam discovered that God can be trusted. God is good. In the midst of death, God is good. When your soul has been cut from your side, your trunk split into two, God is good. All the time. All the time. God is good.

Grief continues, but it also changes, morphs, even softens. But it does not end. Your mate is yours until death parts you both.

I moved away from St. Paul's last year [2005], three years after Laura died. I left Chestertown and Rock Hall and the Eastern Shore. Now I miss the geese on the pond, and my friends at the little church in the country. I miss my walks through the churchyard on the lonely afternoons when up was the wrong direction. But I still walk through the churchyard. I still encounter death as life's shadow, Sheol.

Wherever else Laura may be, Laura lives now in my shadow, and I still see her. And not just as a part of me, and not just as a dream. I look at Tate and I see Laura's jawline and mouth, her big eyes and intensity. And I see in Tilly little pieces, those moments when Laura told Tilly time and again, "Forever and always I will love you," and she pressed the kiss she'd given the inside of Tilly's hand to Tilly's cheek to remind her. Tilly still presses her palm to her cheek. Forever and always. But as I said before, eternity is not found solely in those who follow us—it is found, paradoxically in the cross, in death itself. Life in death.

No, my resurrection story is not the one I imagined, of a second life, another chance. Sam is my resurrection story. Not a change in life, but a change in quality. Of depth. Of understanding. Of trust. I've touched something, and I can't go back.

Solitude—not loneliness—has become a holy friend. A friend I met while walking through the churchyard. Day after day. Month after month. Year after year. A good place to die. A holy place.

EPILOGUE

Just lost when I was saved!
Just felt the world go by!
Just girt me for the onset with eternity,
when breath blew back,
And on the other side,
I heard recede the disappointed tide!

FROM "LITTLE COUSINS, CALLED BACK" BY EMILY
DICKINSON

I dreamed of Laura. Her face was close to mine; only not like it was the last time. The very last time when I tried to wake her from sleep that was death. When I put my nose to her nose, my mouth to her mouth, knowing death was hers, but hoping it wasn't. Not like that.

Rather, she was Laura. My Laura. Beautiful and now somehow pure, her face floating close to mine, a foot away, perhaps. Then closer. I sensed Tate and Tilly nearby, but they were quiet. Watching.

And as Laura looked into my eyes, and I looked into hers, for a flash, for eternity, we were fully intimate, our souls naked to one another, and it was complete and full love—a touching, a being together, as though for one more time, we were one.

Then she pulled back and disappeared. Like a ghost, she fled to another room. I chased her. Down a hallway. Right, then left, then right again. I reached out to her, and finally, I caught her. Only it wasn't Laura this time; it was something else.

"Where's Laura?" I asked.

And this being said simply, "She sent me."

I don't dream of Laura often. Some people dream often of those who have died. Not me. But the other night I dreamed that Laura and I were making love. Almost. We were almost making love. She was beside me, the wisp of her soul. It was familiar, and holy. The warmth of the dream stayed with me. Laura stayed with me.

But Laura's eternity is something other than my dreams. Her eternity is found somehow in a home in another world, and these dreams are but flash photographs taken in that world. Death is a three-day separation, a moment of absence. But eternity is beyond the veil now rent side from side, torn top to bottom. Eternity lay beyond the grave.

"O God, the King eternal, whose light divides the day from the night and turns the shadow of death into the morning…"(Book of Common Prayer, p. 99). It is a shadow, death. In the Old Testament times, those dead were in *Sheol*, a shadow place, not completely gone, but not fully alive. We imagine resurrection life rushed. Someone dies; they are in heaven today. Maybe. Or maybe they, too, are waiting, waiting, waiting for that day when the trumpet sounds, and a voice shouts, and the huge brass door with its enormous ring opens into an Oz world of emerald and gold and life everlasting, welcoming those in the shadow and those still alive to a home that is the home they sought on the earth but never really found, the home that is a home for a soul disjoined from its Creator and sustainer and redeemer.

Laura's home, perhaps, awaits her as it awaits me. It awaits the trumpet of triumph of a King eternal whose shout and light will drive the shadow of death into a permanent light of a sun eternal.

Where there is waterskiing. Where there is chocolate and German beer. Where there is laughter. Where there is life and friends and joy and family. There, where Laura will be, and so will you and me and those we loved.

1805283R00073

Made in the USA
San Bernardino, CA
02 February 2013